HOW TO BE A SUCCESSFUL WIDOW

HOW TO BE A
SUCCESSFUL
WIDOW

By

R. LOUIS ZALK

INTRODUCTION BY

MRS. DALE CARNEGIE

FLEET PUBLISHING CORPORATION

NEW YORK

Library of Congress Catalog Card No. 57-13070

Printed in the United States of America

This effort is dedicated to those it is intended to help, and to those who helped me discharge a self-imposed obligation that was not easy, but immensely gratifying.

CONTENTS

CONTENTS

INTRODUCTION

Perhaps you, like so many other women, used to think that becoming a widow was the sort of thing that only happened to other people. I know that this was my attitude before I lost my husband; and my first days of widowhood were consequently spent in a state of dazed shock which is, I am sure, familiar to most of you who read this.

To all women who lose their husbands, these first days and weeks of widowhood are tragic, whether the marriage that preceded them was brief or of many years' duration. They bring with them not only the grief of losing a beloved husband, but also bewilderment and a pressing need for adjustment to a totally different kind of life.

For all of us, this means adjusting to loneliness, the single responsibility of making decisions for ourselves and our children, if any; and for many of us it may also inv~~~~~~~ancial hardship. But whether we have the financial problem or not, we will all be faced with the need to assume management of our own life, after having shared that management with the person who has protected and sheltered us in the past.

Mr. Zalk's wise and realistic book will prove an invaluable aid during this painful time of grief and everyday adjustment. It provides practical, down-to-earth advice on all aspects of widowhood—particularly the financial and legal aspect which is often so puzzling to women who have had no prior experience in this phase of life. The constructive approach of Mr. Zalk's text will also do much to lift the burden of grief and despair and to inspire you with a sense of new purpose and direction.

When my husband died, I was faced with a great many problems, large and small: the assumption of management of his international business; the many legal and financial aspects of his estate; his other business activities; and the rearing of our four-year-old daughter. I found that in fulfilling these duties and responsibilities, I gained purpose and direction—a worthwhile aim in life.

I was particularly fortunate in the type of business life I inherited when my husband died. His work, which I once shared with him, and which is now mine alone, involves a great deal of contact with other people. The understanding of their diverse problems requires an outgoing personality, and interest and sympathy for their troubles and their aims. I was so busy that I had no time to brood about loneliness.

I was fortunate, too, in having a four-year-old daughter who needed my companionship, guidance, and love. Between my business and my child, my hours were filled with constructive activity.

Whenever possible, I suggest that you, too, try to find a type of career which leaves you no time for self-pity and brooding—a business which deals with the many problems of others, or an activity which keeps you in sympathetic contact with people. Perhaps, in the many case histories which Mr. Zalk presents in this book, you will be aided in redeveloping your interest in your fellowmen and the life that continues to go on around you.

Fully as important to you is the knowledge that you are not alone in your sorrows and problems—that they are being shared and overcome by thousands of women in every country every day. This book will help you to realize that the death of your husband does not mean the end of your life. True, a most important chapter of your life has drawn to a close; but this book can be an instrument in opening up the next chapter for you—a chapter of life that will be full of rich and rewarding achievement.

Mrs. Dale Carnegie

PREFACE

MRS. DALE CARNEGIE finds herself in the same situation as many thousands of other women in this country and abroad. The statistics on this point are formidable. Every year, approximately half a million wives become widows, about half as many husbands become widowers, and more than one-third of a million dependent children become orphans. Nearly seventy per cent of the children become the sole responsibility of mothers. In the early years of this century, widows were increasing by fewer than 80,000 annually. But since 1930, the yearly increase has been about 100,-000. And the indication is that the number of widows will continue to increase—probably to 8.5 million by 1960 as compared with approximately 7.5 million now.

I have been acutely aware of the magnitude and extent of the problem of widowhood for close to two decades, and have done constant research on the subject and all its ramifications since.

My interest in the problems of widows grew out of experiences on a personal level. The deaths of a number of my relatives, friends, and business associates brought home to me the great plight, both material

11

and spiritual, in which they left their wives. Many of these newly bereaved widows turned to me for assistance and advice. In my effort to help I was amazed at the lack of readily available facts and material. I determined to remedy this situation as soon as possible, and out of this attempt grew my newspaper column "How to Be a Successful Widow." Ever since then, I have been completely absorbed by the problem of widowhood which has become the dominant interest of my life. My experience in the field is being constantly enriched and broadened by the tremendous amount of mail I receive from persons all over the country, of every walk of life and every economic class.

One of the surprising aspects that has emerged through this correspondence is that men also are deeply concerned with the subject of widowhood— either for themselves, or for the wives they would some day leave behind them. I have always tried to answer all these letters to the best of my ability, and have been grateful for the opportunity they afforded me to delve deeper and deeper into my subject.

You will therefore find very little ivory-tower theory in this book. Apart from a few basic statistics, all the material is the direct outgrowth of my experiences and relationships with my numerous readers. This seemed to me the best guarantee that what I have to say in these pages will apply to you as it does to so many others, and will afford you a measure of help and solace.

R. L. ZALK

CARRYING ON GRACEFULLY

You made concessions when you accepted wifehood, further concessions if you also entered motherhood. You must concede in widowhood too, with all the good grace that you can muster. Then, you will improve your own ideas and ideals of self-respect, and you will gain greatly in the estimation of all those who are concerned for you. Others—millions of widows— have achieved these goals. "Go thou and do likewise."

Lonesomeness! What does it mean? The widow needs no dictionary definition to explain the meaning of this word. Very soon in her new situation, she learns from actual experience all that this abstract term cannot convey on printed paper. She need not be told that the three elements which enter into the making of this word (lone-some-ness) signify, "sad from lack of companionship or sympathy."

13

Unfriended! Unvisited! Uninvited! Unintroduced! Left to shift for herself because she lost her biological standing when she lost her husband. Being no longer married, but still in a sense married, her status seems to be midway between that of the single woman and that of the married woman—which leaves her neither here nor there, so to speak.

In the course of gathering information for this book I have interviewed many widows for the purpose of probing their principal problems. As a result, I realized that in the main—following a period of readjustment—their main problem is lonesomeness.

A great number of communications which have reached me from widows all over the country attest to this:

"I am 30 years old and have been a widow for two years. I am attractive and have always enjoyed various sports. I liked my home until my husband died. I realize that being alone has had something to do with my feelings, but I am so lonely all the time. I can't seem to shake off this feeling.

"The married couples my husband and I knew are just as nice as ever. But I feel so out of place with them. I have often thought that if I could meet some nice man I would not be lonely. But at my age most men are married, and I certainly would not want to have dates with a married man. How can I go about meeting someone?"

"I am a lonely woman. Am I a nuisance and neurotic because I want the companionship of a man? And not just any man either?

"I am 32 and have been a widow for over three years;

and I haven't met a single man yet who was in his forties. I suppose there are widowers and bachelors, but I don't know any of them.

"I feel like an old hen. What can I do?"

"I have been a widow for four years. I dress nicely and converse well. I work and so do not have much time for recreation. I am 39, and a lady in every respect. I would do my part for a real home and a nice husband."

"When I was in my early thirties I was left a widow with three children. Now, ten years later, my children are practically grown and I am pretty much alone.

"I have a good position, but I crave companionship. I do not go out in the evenings, therefore I never meet men. I am not interested in men my age for they usually like younger girls. Older men appeal to me because I am the stay-at-home type.

"What do you suggest as a solution to my problem?"

"I wish you would tell me how to meet a man of about 45 or 50 years of age.

"Is there some organization I could write to in order to find someone to whom I could write? The work I do doesn't supply me with proper friends. I am 45 and very lonely."

"My problem is loneliness. Since the death of my husband two years ago I live alone, renting my upstairs to an older woman.

"I work in an office where the women are around 60. I am 29 and all I do is work and go home.

"It seems as if I never have anyone to go with. I am satisfied to work, but I would like to enjoy a few pleasures. At my age men are very scarce.

"My heart almost breaks when the holidays come around. Most people look forward to them, but I feel they are only something to be endured, and I am glad when they are over.

"I become so desperate. I try to be friendly and have a good many friends, but they are all married and this does me no good when I want to enjoy a little life.

"I do so want to change my life and outlook, but I do not know how to go about it.

"Can you help me?"

It must be noted that the women who wrote these letters were in their thirties and forties. They had been wives who were just becoming accustomed to the meaning of marriage, or who had reached that stage in their natural and in their married lives when thought of any other mode of existence was remote as regards the past, and repulsive as regards the future. Then a stroke of fate constrained them to accept a state of solitude which is singular to the widow.

Then, after a period of readjustment lasting two to three years in the average case, a rebellion arises which cannot be quelled. Inherent feminine instincts and needs cause her to crave the companionship of a man. That is the character of each complaint and the theme-tone of all. They sound a note of striking sameness which inspires solicitude. What advice may be given to them that may provide an alternative?

First, would it not be well for a lonely window to try to subdue her yearning through sublimation, that is, try to elevate her mind above an interest in men through substitution of a perhaps worthier interest? In many instances, as will be illustrated later, "a man in her life" may not tend to improve her materially, but to injure her morally.

Relieved of the requirements of wifehood, and often of the responsibilities of motherhood also, a widow many devote much of her time and of her thinking to a program of self-improvement, or to altruistic activities.

If she is obliged to work to support herself in whole or in part, she may invest her spare time in preparing herself for an advanced position offering more money —a means of providing more satisfactorily for today's requirements and tomorrow's security. Thus she may train herself for a new, absorbing, remunerative career, in a new field of opportunity. While so engaged, she may even meet a man able to supply her with a satisfactory measure of masculine companionship.

On the other hand, propinquity may serve to stimulate rather than ease her propensity. Some sapient soul has said, "There is no such thing as a platonic friendship." And many men adopt the view, "What harm can it do, as long as it's *play* for me and *tonic* for her?"

A woman of character will not permit herself to become the "play" thing of any man. From the long view, from the short view, from any point of view, it is something she cannot afford to do. She may have to manage with spare clothing, second-rate food, and shabby shelter, but shoddy companionship is something she can shun.

What of the widow of wealth, she who has perhaps

too much money in her hands and too much time on her hands—how may she elude loneliness? Charitable and civic enterprises offer her the ideal means of expending her time and money. What she may lack of talent for this purpose will be compensated for by sincere interest. All she needs is incentive. Once she devotes herself to the welfare of those less fortunate, she will find this an all-absorbing mission.

"How can I go about meeting someone?" asks the first of the six "lonesomeness" letters presented in these pages. The academic answer would be, "Let Nature take its course." But Nature at times has a way of remaining idle. So it may be more politic to heed the practical proverb which points out that, "God helps those who help themselves." In short, the widow who covets masculine companionship should "sell" herself, in the virtuous sense of the word, of course. And subtly!

A selling campaign, like a military campaign, calls for strategy and tactics; first, for predetermined planning, and second, for skillful maneuvering in the presence of the prospect.

Successful selling involves certain fundamental procedures: 1. Location of a logical market for the product. 2. Proper presentation in various attractive ways. 3. Exposure to likely prospects. When a widow wants to meet suitable men, her campaign should follow similar steps. Be her ultimate goal a husband, or just a congenial companion, the project calls for these procedures: 1. A mental picture of men who would appeal to her and to whom she might appeal. 2. Personal attractiveness pitched to the highest degree. 3. Natural or contrived opportunity to mingle among such men. If this counsel seems too coldly calculating for the romanticist to accept without question, she must remember that definite purposes demand definite procedures.

This would seem to be a suitable place to say something about the Cheer Up Club of Columbus, Ohio, a social organization which has received a great deal of favorable publicity during the several years of its existence. Membership is limited to widows, spinsters, and bachelors who are more than 45 years of age. While the members dine and dance and make merry at their monthly meetings, one suspects that the principal purpose of these get-togethers is to provide opportunity for the members to meet prospective mates. Making the Cheer Up Club the subject of one of his avidly read columns, Johnny Jones, a popular writer for the *Columbus Dispatch*, and himself a bachelor, wrote:

The other night there were forty women and eleven men at the party. There you have a pretty fair average, but terrific competition. The president of the club, a lovely lady, is enormously popular. I saw a lot of the boys trying to catch her eye and if she does not look out, she may marry an outsider and that would be cause for immediate impeachment.

They tell of three happy marriages that originated at the jolly meetings of their club. You cannot continue to attend meetings if you marry someone who is not a member of the club.

The men get real attention. There's no sign of rheumatism or neuritis among the members. At least they will not admit it. You would be surprised to know what well-known women are members of the club. One is the house mother of a prominent sorority at the University.

Many members have been married and have grown children. It's funny though. Nobody comes to get them. They either make a date with one of the men or go alone. They spot a romance starting, quicker than a bird dog can spot a rabbit trail.

The dues are only ten cents. That would not keep anyone away. I had more fun at this party than I ever had at a circus. But I must be slipping or I haven't the right technique, for I couldn't make a date or get a telephone number at the Cheer Up Club.

If there isn't an organization like the Cheer Up Club in her community, perhaps some enterprising widow should undertake to institute the idea for the benefit of other lonely persons, as well as for herself. Properly conducted, such a social club is a most commendable venture.

Contrasting the praiseworthy fellowship offered by an organization such as the Cheer Up Club, is the questionable service performed by the matrimonial agency. The one is organized to foster fine friendship —a kind of love that is not primarily involved with flowers and veils. The other is essentially a commercial enterprise which, for some sort of fee, seeks to establish contacts between men and women that may lead to a correspondence courtship and a mail-order consortship.

There is no disgrace in being a widow, but many widows certainly disgrace themselves in many ways in matters of conduct and attitude. And mismanagement of money, mis-matched marriage, futile martyrdom and melancholia are not the only ways. There is also the matter of moral conduct to consider. There are widows of seemingly impeccable character, as well as those of ill-repute, who accept the attentions of even married men, in order to have a love life. Sometimes these infatuations are of long duration; sometimes of short season.

Anyone who attempts to build himself up by tearing another down, is a reprehensible person. Certainly, a widow who errs in this way cannot hope to re-establish her own home by breaking another woman's heart and home. These irregular relationships, these potentially scandalous affairs, carried on surreptitiously in some "cheaters' paradise," cannot possibly give the participating parties the satisfactions which stem from sanctioned love.

Sad to say, there are widows who form an attachment for no one man, but who "play the field," as it is said.

Concerning one such woman, her own daughter bitterly complains:

"My mother is disgracing us. I am so ashamed of her, I can hardly face my family and friends.

"Father wasn't buried a month before she started having dates with men. And what men! Old, young, married, single, any kind.

"She drinks and smokes, which are things she never did before, and she spends all her time in liquor places. She doesn't care where she goes or who she goes with. One night my husband found her in a cheap night spot with a young hoodlum. He had to fight them both to get her out of the place.

"Sometimes she has dates with traveling men and stays away all night. Once she went out of town with some unknown man. We found out when she wired for money to get back home.

"She is 47. What a way for a woman of that age to act! We are afraid of what may happen to her."

The daughter wants to know what to do with this middle-aged, mischief-making mother. One need not be a professional psychologist to see what is behind this woman's behavior. Even a cursory investigation was enough to confirm the conjectures of an interested person's insight.

In her girlhood, the woman was a vivacious, flirtatious hoyden. Fearing she would disgrace herself, her family managed to marry her off to a rather staid and settled bank clerk who was senior to her by almost ten years. During the thirty-one years of their married life she led an exemplary existence out of respect to everyone concerned in the situation. But when her husband died, the major restraining influence was relaxed. Pent up propensities were released, and she literally "went wild."

Others may misbehave, but children want a mother

to be beyond reproach in the matter of morals. It may do no good to plead with this woman. Perhaps the best solution to the problem she has created is to have her confined to a sanatorium until she regains her better sense. But before resorting to such a drastic measure, it might be well for the daughter to try to supply her mother's need for excitement with home entertainment. In time, this woman, with the help of her family, could regain control of herself. In a sense she is ill. Illness requires treatment, and drastic measures should not be employed before mild treatment has been tried.

Estelle's sorrow for her husband was sharp, but of short duration—like pain following a kick in the shins. Due to his lifelong emotional instability, he wasn't the easiest man in the world to live with. Their friends and his co-workers thought there was something "seriously wrong" with him, but tolerated him to the extent necessary.

He entertained an avid ambition to be a major executive in the company that employed him, but his ability and attitude were far short of even the essential requirements. When the position he wanted most went to a co-worker who was deemed worthy of the responsibility, he went to pieces. Eventually he did away with himself.

Soon, Estelle was going out on occasional dates with a well-to-do bachelor who was approaching middle age. The fellow was tall, stark, and gruesome, but his prominent position in the business world and his passion for spending money freely obscured, in her eyes, his uncomeliness.

Estelle met her friend through mutual friends, a couple who liked to "live it up," and who had a host of friends who looked at life the same way. Eventually, he was expected to escort Estelle to certain social affairs to which she was invited, and she was always available when his invitations said or read "and lady." In the course of time, they became a steady twosome, and their friends were beginning to wonder when they would be receiving invitations to a wedding.

She was aware that her "Bachelor of Silence" had a habit of attaching himself to widows and divorcees until he wore out his welcome. She was anxious to marry him, but he was absolutely noncommittal. Living in hope and afraid of losing him, Estelle let things drift—for eleven years. The thing that brought things to a head was the fact that Estelle's daughter had just graduated from college. Her friend paid no attention to the girl at any time. As far as he was concerned, the child didn't exist.

He did not accept an invitation to attend the graduation exercises, nor did he extend the customary congratulations or send a suitable gift. That settled the situation for Estelle. As far as she was concerned, she was through. Finished!

The purpose of presenting this case history is not to probe the mind of the man who attached himself to her for so many years with no idea of marrying her.

The purpose is to point up that there are many such men and many widows who accept their attentions to the point of absurdity. Some of those women are due for a rude awakening.

There are fairly well-to-do widows, women who are fair of face and fair of form, who "accidentally" attach themselves to fairly "well-heeled" and well-connected old bachelors in the hope of contracting another advantageous alliance.

Thereupon they enter into a little game called "Put n' Take," which seems to have no ending. She gives without stint, and he takes without conscience, the comforts of her home, the competence of her cooking, the flattery of her attention, the adulation of her acquaintances. If she has children, they only irritate him when he cannot ignore them. For months, often for years, he revels in a relationship that provides all of the prerequisites to marriage, as well as most, if not all of the perquisites and prerogatives that go with wedlock. All this, but without any responsibilities of his own.

At long last, the widow may tire of "putting" and decide to "take." Unable to maneuver him into a proposal, she proposes marriage herself. He stalls her off with a series of stale excuses, then eventually vanishes into the embrace of another waiting widow—grass or sod, as opportunity affords.

In presenting these experiences, the author cannot be accused of casting aspersion upon widows, individually or collectively, for each account, each statement, each summary is fact or based on fact. The reader is reminded that the sole purpose of this book is to alert, to admonish, and to advise.

A bit of good advice is here offered by a woman of 35 who has been a widow for eight years:

"My husband was a wonderful man and we were very much in love. Perhaps I expect too much of the man I wish to make a home for, but in all this time I haven't met one who measures up to my ideals.

"I think the old saying, 'Better to have loved and lost than never to have loved at all,' is completely wrong. Perhaps I would be happier not knowing what I am missing now.

"Because I have been a widow eight years, even my family doctor thinks I must be lax in morals, and the boss where I work thinks I should let him do as he pleases and be grateful for small favors.

"All the men I meet seem to want all the personal liberties with no responsibility, and this doesn't fit in with my upbringing or my ideals."

What this wise woman is saying is that she is not available to any man who has not as much to offer *morally* as she has. Every widow is well advised to consider carefully the intentions of every man who approaches her. "See where you stand *before you fall*," is a safeguarding slogan for her to keep in mind. There is no point in taking any more punishment than is necessary.

It is completely natural for a normal woman to have need of a man, just as for physical reasons she has need of food and sleep. Her need is for sex relations as well as for companionship. The power of this attraction is due to the activity of the sex glands. It is this potent force which perpetuates the human race. As in men, the impulse is stronger in some women than it is in others. And at certain periods in the life span, the desire is more acute than at other times, due to stimulation or cessation of gland activity, as the case may be. To satisfy sexual desire, hers and her fiancé's, a woman marries. Whether marriage results in mere legal cohabitation or life-long love, she becomes habituated to sexual relations, whose sudden cessation causes restlessness.

While sleep researchers claim that only 16 per cent of the world's people know how to relax completely, the author ventures the observation that there is less insomnia among well-mated married couples than there is among any other class of persons of adult age. Then what relief is there for the woman who has lived with a man for ten, twenty, or thirty years, and who is suddenly denied the sedative effect of satisfactory sexual intercourse? She should give heed to tested ideas which induce relaxation and sound slumber.

Counting sheep and similar ideas are old standbys. Warm milk taken at bed time is scientifically approved. Planned mental and physical exercise will counteract restlessness, and induce repose, as will certain soporific drugs, which should be taken under the direction of a doctor. Reading oneself to sleep is another time-tested remedy.

The experience of the woman who enters the menopause at the same time that she enters widowhood, is trying indeed. Such a woman must be extremely vigilant in exercising the care that is essential for the preservation of her health—especially if she is a mother of dependent children. All too often, she is neglectful of herself while giving ungrudgingly of herself to her fatherless family. Vanishing vitality begins to take a terrific toll of health and happiness. All but consumed by work and worry, she is poorly prepared to cope with the ravages of time and trouble. During this dire period, a skillful doctor may do much to alleviate any distress and disturbance that may accompany the climacteric. And much of his practice is devoted to dealing with the deteriorations that are an attendant circumstance of advancing age. But in over-taxing themselves, women often over-tax the ability of the most competent physician. Consciously or unconsciously, but nonetheless certainly, they enter upon a critical period of life, without concern for the care which they owe themselves—not only for personal reasons, but also for the sake of their children and society in general.

Fortified with common sense and with vigor, a widow may face the future philosophically and with fortitude. Living gracefully, with consideration for self, she will live usefully, providing not only the care and comfort required by her children but also the counsel and the companionship that are indispensable to children bereft of a father.

CHAPTER II

ORIENTATION TO WIDOWHOOD

Currently, about two-thirds of a million marriages are broken annually—by death.

Generally, a father's death imposes serious economic hardship on his survivors. That is especially evident when the father succumbs at an early age. Although the likelihood of suffering an early death is comparatively small, still about one hundred thousand dependent children a year lose fathers who were under forty-five years of age.

In recent years, much has been done to help alleviate the financial strain which loss of the principal breadwinner imposes on a broken family, but in countless cases, the burden brought to bear on the mothers of orphaned children is distressing. A two-fold responsibility—a double problem—is forced upon them:

29

that of providing and that of maintaining a home, for years may pass before the children become partially or totally self-supporting.

Each year, the largest group of orphans—more than eighty thousand—derives from fathers who die during midlife. Since most of the children are in their late teens and approaching the age when they could be gainfully employed, the financial strain on many families will be less acute. However, there will be cases in which a measure of financial support as well as maternal supervision will be required. And no doubt many children will find it necessary to revise their educational ambitions.

The number of dependent orphans resulting from the deaths of mothers is approximately half the number of those who lose their fathers. The widower with minor children also faces problems peculiar to his new situation. Generally, he is away from home earning a living, but in being able to earn a living, he is able to provide a hired housekeeper for his family, if he is unable or unwilling to find another wife.

Although the stability and well-being of American family life has improved materially as a result of the continued decline in mortality, the untimely death of parents will be with us always, and that of fathers will be predominant. Therefore, I would say to all the husbands and wives of America—especially those who are parents of dependent children:

HOPE FOR THE BEST, BUT BE PREPARED FOR THE WORST.

Save systematically. Spend wisely. Swat the "squander bug" unhesitatingly. Build some kind of reliable financial bulwark for the protection of your family, even if eventually it consists only of an aging widow or widower. Safeguarded by a measure of financial security, survivors can face the future with a measure of equanimity and fortitude.

Why are there more widows than widowers? More than three times as many, as a matter of fact? Is it because there are more women than men? That would seem to supply a pat answer, but it's only part of the answer.

The marital statistics show that in March, 1956 there were about 38.3 million husbands and 38.3 million wives living together, including members of the Armed Forces living off post. On that score, what is sauce for the goose is sauce for the gander. But the same report indicated that there were 7.7 million widows to 2.3 million widowers. Why the dreadful disparity?

Well, women seem to have a biological advantage from the start. The ratio at birth is 106 baby boys to 100 baby girls, but from birth on, it is a statistical fact that women live longer than men.

Today, in general, women live about six years longer than men and some wives outlive their husbands by 20 years or more.

There was a time back in the 1940s when there were more men than women, but the proportion of men has been dropping steadily since 1910.

The trend was accelerated by the amazing advances

in medical progress against diseases which affect women more severely than men.

The virtual elimination of the risks of childbearing and the immense improvement in the standard of living exerted additional beneficial effects.

The result has meant the addition of years to the lives of women. Men, too, are living longer, but as people advance in age, the difference in longevity between the sexes becomes greater.

"The years between 45 and 60 are particularly dangerous for men," states a reputable family physician, "whereas women find the going harder after 80."

Another factor to take into account is the accident death rate with respect to married persons. The ratio in a recent year was 3.3 men to one woman.

The higher toll among men reflects their greater exposure to hazards, and their greater daring.

Bachelors, obviously, aren't killing themselves to provide a better world for their wives, yet their death rate is almost two-thirds higher than that of married men.

Married people experience a lower mortality than those who remain single and those whose marriage was broken by death or divorce.

In the main, marriage is more beneficial than harmful to mankind.

It's just that men are more fragile and more exposed to fatal accidents than women. Perhaps that's why there are more widows than widowers.

GENTLEMEN BEFORE LADIES

Birth is the harbinger of death. As soon as we are born, we begin to die. But with respect to longevity, generally it's a case of "Gentlemen Before Ladies," for women outlive men, wives outlive husbands.

The probability that a wife will survive her husband depends on the difference in their ages. It increases with the number of years she is younger than her husband. When they are the same age, the chances that she will survive him are 60 in 100. But they rise to 70 when the husband is five years older, and almost to 80 if he is senior to her by ten years.

Widowhood is practically a certainty for wives who are 20 or more years younger than their husbands, the probability in such cases being 90 in 100. Only if the wife is at least five years older than her husband are the odds against her becoming a widow.

A census report released December 21, 1956, indicated there were about 60.1 million females in our population who were 14 years of age and older. Approximately 7.7 million—1 in every 8—were widows. Natural widows, not divorcees. Close to 10 per cent of all the families in the United States are headed by widows. Numbering about 4.7 million, they account for what may be termed the largest group of broken families in the nation.

Thus, the possibility of a wife becoming a widow is inescapable. Yet, though the fact is generally recognized, it is not likely that the average, normal woman prepares herself for the possibility of widowhood with as much interest and intelligence as she prepares herself for wifehood and motherhood. Enjoying some measure of financial security, social position, and connubial satisfaction, the married woman seldom thinks of the possibility of becoming a widow.

If she does occasionally, the thought is banished from her mind as quickly and as completely as possible. What sort of a life would she live, what sort of a wife would she be if she gave constant thought to the most grievous of all thoughts? For it is natural for a wife to think of life and love, unnatural for her to think of death and distress. Not until she is obliged to contend with the strange, trying, critical problems that are peculiar to her changed position and condition, does a widowed woman recognize a need for some source of reliable, readily available information that will help her meet and manage a new way of life.

A sincere attempt was made in this book to assemble, sort, refine, and interpret those matters that would be of major and vital importance to her, keeping in mind the traditions of widowhood, so that she may understand the influence of the past as well as the effect of the present on her hopes, plans, and aspirations.

MOURNING

Mourning originated with the primitive notion that those who were present at death should be shunned. Death was thought to be contagious. Those present at death were regarded as unclean and apt to contaminate others. The masquerade of mourning was meant as a disguise against evil spirits. It was also meant to serve as a warning that the wearers were "unclean."

Definite and dire were the prejudices, prohibitions, and ostracisms which uncivilized men inflicted on the mourners in their midst, especially women. For a woman, particularly a widow, was expected to mourn more than a man. She was regarded as a chattel secured to cater to his creature comforts. Therefore, she was compelled to continue to serve him as chief mourner.

When death became involved with superstition is not known. What is worth knowing is when man first started the slow process of shedding the appalling practices which encrusted him for centuries. There is no sure answer. Only speculation.

There is nothing dictated in any form of Christian religion that sanctioned some funeral rites. Through one pretext or another, they were foisted upon fearful minds and persisted so long that they came to have the force of common law. As far as ceremony is concerned, the Catholic Church applies to those deceased only those rites which are enjoined for the living. Nor can we fasten upon Judaism what remains of pagan funeral practices. Simplicity was enjoined for a people who naturally love display. It was strictly ordained that anything in the nature of ostentation was to be omitted from the funeral service. During prescribed times, periods, and in stated places, the survivors recall the departed to memory with recitation of Kaddish prayers.

The first solemn protestation against mourning garments came from the Society of Friends (Quakers). Practicing remarkable simplicity in all matters, these spiritual people deemed it absurd to wear black garments for those whom they believed had put on everlasting white. The majority of early Methodists held the same considered opinion, though in less positive form. Uncivilized peoples believed that when they were cloaked or veiled in black, they were invisible to evil spirits and free of any possibility of molestation. Among civilized peoples, black was considered most becoming for expressing the feelings of a soul abandoned to grief.

From the standpoint of costume and color, black has become objectionable because it has lost most, if not all of the sacred significance it once had. It is no longer a mark of mourning. It is and has been high-style for many seasons, a color capable of expressing vanity as well as grief.

Whether mourning is to be considered a means of showing respect for the departed, or securing a modicum of solace for oneself, discharging a sacred duty, or displaying personal decorum, it is a matter in which another may not meddle. Should a question of this nature arise, it must be answered in the heart and in the mind of the person who is directly concerned.

In the words of an old proverb: "If you sing, you

cannot mourn; if you mourn, you cannot sing." Few customs have changed as radically in recent years as those which constrained a mourner, especially a widow, with respect to dress and demeanor. Time was when a widow's prescribed costume and enjoined manner of behavior had a profound purpose. They were intended to provide her with a measure of protection from work-a-day intrusions, as well as a means of commemoration. Every stitch of the dismal outer garments worn by widows of middle and advanced age was made of materials and in a manner meant to denote proper decorum. For street wear, they would put on a small black bonnet with a widow's cap-border made of white crepe. Covering the face and extending to the lower edge of the skirt in front and back, they wore an affair made of nun's veiling. At the termination of three months, they were permitted to fasten the front veil back from the face. Frequently worn for life, the long veil was worn for at least two years. Today, people would look askance at such vesture, even if it were worn by widows of greatly advanced age.

Younger widows were not exempted from periods of primary and secondary mourning and the manner of their garments was rigidly circumscribed. For economic reasons, many of them remarried quickly and often frequently. It was not obligatory for them to continue in conventional mourning upon accepting the attentions of a prospective new provider.

Today, a widow makes her own decisions regarding

what she will wear in the way of mourning attire, if any, and for how long. She realizes that her conduct is of far greater signifiance than her costume.

Frequently, a widow wants to know if it is correct for her to use the title "Mrs." in connection with her given name. Socially, it is never correct for her to do so. The title "Mrs." is significant. It is the equivalent of "wife," or "wed to." Therefore, it is used only in connection with her late husband's first name or names, or with the initials indicative of those names. For formal use, the proper form is "Mrs. Samuel S. Smith." Informally, she should sign herself "Susan Smith." For legal purposes, usually, "(Mrs.) Susan Smith."

"Is it inexcusable not to acknowledge each message of sympathy?" widows have asked. Obviously, if circumstances permit, it is obligatory to respond to a message of condolence. A short, simple, sincere note of appreciation will suffice. If the list is long, another person may make the acknowledgements, preferably a member of the family.

Some widows wonder if they should use mourning stationery upon which to write acknowledgements. The practice has practically disappeared. Plain white paper of fine quality may be used. And black ink, of course. Engraved or finely printed cards are quite proper in cases where the deceased was a prominent public personage, and where a large number of messages of sympathy were received, including many from persons not known personally to the widow.

In the normal course of events, a widow is not expected to return calls of sympathy, not even when extremely helpful service has been rendered. The social significance of such calls would be small indeed. Common sense constrains custom to defer to her.

Occasionally, queries come from confused women who are separated, but not divorced, from their husbands. What is the obligation of the separatee to the deceased and the members of his family? Considering such a case in all its aspects, it would seem there are no midway measures that would satisfy both her own conscience and the requirements of convention. She should regard herself as a member of the family with certain reservations, or as a complete stranger, and conduct herself accordingly.

Another in the category of perplexing problems is this: What arrangements should be made for the christening of a child that was born after the death of its father? Common sense would counsel that arrangements be of the utmost simplicity in all respects.

What should a widow do with the rings symbolic of her first betrothal and marriage when she becomes engaged to marry again? After she has received her second engagement ring, it would hardly be right to continue to wear those rings, especially if she has any regard for the feelings of her fiancé.

What kind of a wedding may a widow have when she remarries? Again, common sense counsels elimination of everything of an elaborate nature, even for a widow who is quite young. Simplicity and informality—those are the watchwords.

The essence of etiquette is consideration. When one is in doubt about any matter of conventional conduct, she will not go far wrong if she will use common sense to resolve an unfamiliar situation. That implies consideration for all others involved, as well as for oneself.

A bereaved family is often beset with fears of one kind and another. Not many young children are frightened by death, or disturbed by bereavement. They are too immature to understand the significance of what has happened. When they do become disturbed, it is because the adults in the family abandon themselves to open grief and carry the children with them. The effect of adult affliction on the minds of young children may be definitely detrimental.

To avoid injury to an extent, and entirely if possible, it is advisable to ask relatives, close friends, or kindly neighbors to take such children into their homes until the adults recover themselves.

Few parents are aware of it, but one of the principal causes of fear in immature children is rooted in the reason that they are dependent on their parents for almost everything. When their breadwinner is taken from them, they begin to wonder: what will happen to me? Will I have to quit school? Will I have to go to work? What can I do? What can I earn?

It is the distorted worries of youth that eventuate

in the most appalling of all human anxieties—the dread of death. As soon as she is able to do so, the mother should inform her children how the family will fare financially. It is always best to face facts and it is best to face them together. To dispel the fears of a child regarding death, the mother or some one who understands should make an effort to explain that there is nothing mysterious about a natural demise, or death due to some different cause for that matter.

Until it is understood that dying is the natural dissolution of a person, death cannot be explained to oneself, or to another. It is no different with human life than it is with plant life. A seed is sown . . . the cells develop . . . multiply . . . bud . . . bloom . . . degenerate . . . die. That is the natural course of birth, life, death.

In explaining death to a young child, it would be thoughtful to use a flower as an example, citing each of the processes enumerated, noting that eventually the flower reverts to seed, the means of producing another generation. It would be quite natural to point out that a multitude of flowers are also subject to maladies that result in mortality, and that many are also cut down in their prime or earlier, and to come to an untimely end.

While some tranquil mothers may have turbulent children, it is not likely that irritable mothers will have imperturbable children.

The loss of her husband combined with the vexing problems that attended his passing, may convert a perfectly poised woman into a bundle of nerves, if not a confirmed neurotic. The best way for a nervous mother to heal a nervous child is to deal first with herself. Whatever she may do to evidence control of her own emotions will have a salutary effect on the child.

The widow who is not below par during the early days of her bereavement is the exception. Often, she is adversely affected for weeks or months. The physical aspect of grief manifests itself in impaired body tone due to the impeded action of certain glands. Normally, those glands enrich the blood with enlivening elements. But when a person is in despair, those same organs eliminate some secretions that increase dejection.

During such a trying time, a qualified, understanding doctor may do much to alleviate the distress that accompanies affliction. As a matter of fact, the bereaved woman should undergo a complete physical checkup as soon as she conveniently can. No power can give her a happy hour when health is lost. So what she does have of health must be kept intact, and improved if possible. Even though she be left in extremely modest circumstances and thinks she cannot afford such attention, she must be made to realize that her health is something she cannot afford to neglect.

Especially is this a matter of paramount importance for the 100,000 women who become widowed annually when they are at or under middle life. For it is these younger widows who will have in their care almost all of the younger dependent children who lose their fathers in an average year. The care of dependent children is a great and a grave responsibility, and the widowed mother will need good health as much as she will need anything to cope with her situation. For when a family man leaves this life, it may be said that two men have departed—a father as well as a husband.

Of the 450,000 women who currently enter widowhood in an average year, more than one-fifth are approaching or are already experiencing the menopause, commonly called the change of life period.

An authority has noted that during this period about one-third of the women so affected experience no difficulty, that another third are moderately bothered, and that another third have a trying time of it.

For certain reasons, being without a husband bears most heavily on many of the women in the last-mentioned group. A woman so afflicted may feel like "beating her husband's brains out one day and loving him to distraction the next." A widow has no husband upon whom she may expend these emotions, but she can call upon medical science and skill to help her subdue them.

I am not a medical man, so I may not presume to practice medicine in the public prints. But I may presume, with some propriety, to discuss the matter of choosing a physician.

Now there are doctors and doctors, but regardless of his general or specialized skill, a doctor must have the confidence of his patient in order to accomplish the greatest good. If a patient has any "feeling" about the ability of a doctor, it would be better for both if she found another in whom she felt she could put her faith. But—she must make sure that she receives the attention of an ethical physician and not a quack. Answers to certain questions indicate a doctor's natural aptitude, educational attainment, and professional ability.

Is he a graduate of a recognized medical school? Was his medical training followed by one or two years of internship in a recognized hospital?

Does he have a license granted by the State Board of Registration and Licensure to practice medicine in the State in which he maintains his office?

Is he a member of the County Medical Society, of the State Medical Society, of the American Medical Association, or of any other organized, recognized body of physicians?

It is not difficult to differentiate between the ethical physician and the fraud and the faker. The former maintains a permanent place of practice, avoids advertising and publicity as such, displays his State certificate and perhaps his diplomas on the walls of his office for the assurance of his patients, and he keeps essential identifying-informative signs within the limits of dignified good taste. As for the latter, the quack usually does what the ethical doctor never does.

To a large extent, our early doctors were products of the school of experience. They were admired especially for their ability to practice the art of scientific observation, using to the utmost the five senses supplemented by common sense. They developed friendly personal relationships with their patients. Today, as then, such relationship between physician and patient is regarded as the basic requirement of the best type of medical practice.

Medical science has made amazing strides in recent years. The modern physician, today, has available many devices for supplementing his five senses, but unless brain work—common sense—is used in connection with those devices, the usefulness of the mechanical aids will be impaired.

Find a doctor who uses common sense, and you will usually find one who is conscientious and competent.

CHAPTER III

FINANCIAL AND LEGAL AFFAIRS

"Where ignorance is bliss, 'tis folly to be wise," is a saying that may suit some situations. But it should be ruled out of a marriage relationship if——

If it means keeping either spouse, and especially the wife, in perpetual darkness as regards the family's financial situation. It is an insidious idea which many husbands, both prosperous and comparatively poor, impose on their wives for reasons that are not realistic.

When a concerned wife is relegated to the role of a nonentity with respect to the family's financial affairs, it could put some strain on a marriage that is intact, and an added affliction on her should it be broken by the death of the breadwinner. Nor may a wife absolve herself from permitting such a situation to exist. It is not expedient for her to assume that everything is and will be all right in the event that her husband is called to his Maker.

I believe that I can offer my readers, both husbands and wives, no better advice than this in cases where it applies:

Get together immediately to take stock of where you stand financially. And this: Compile a carefully detailed check list of information that is pertinent. An ordinary 9 x 12 loose-leaf notebook would be best for the purpose.

Include this information:

ADVISERS—List the names of lawyer, financial counsel, and insurance agent, and how to reach each one in an emergency.

INSURANCE—List each policy, kind of insurance provided, company which issued it, the policy number, the amount of insurance, the beneficiary, and the terms of settlement.

EMPLOYMENT RECORD—Note that of the husband (and that of the wife, too, if she is employed) for Social Security purposes. Name the employers, the starting and terminating dates with each employer, and the total earnings received. Note the Social Security number, and estimated monthly payments, including those for children under 18 who might be left in the care of the mother.

BANK ACCOUNTS—List name of each bank, kind of account in each, in whose name or names, and safe deposit number.

SAVINGS BONDS—Note cash and maturity values,

and ownership. List serial numbers and maturity dates.

REAL ESTATE—Give accurate description, value, mortgage, insurance, assessments, and ownership.

SECURITIES—List description, value, yield, and ownership.

CAR—Note make, model, current value, amount owed, insurance, and ownership.

OTHER ASSETS—List, describe, and estimate present value of items worth considering.

DEBTORS AND/OR CREDITORS—List names, amounts due, date due, how and when payable.

VITAL RECORDS—Birth certificates, marriage and divorce records, will of husband and of wife, personal and property insurance policies and premium receipts, deeds to real estate, title to car, securities and savings bonds, military service records, tax receipts, and property improvement records.

Date this record, revise it as required, and keep it in a safe, accessible place.

WIDOWS BEWARE

In the famous fairy tale by Lewis Carrol, Alice falls asleep, and then awakens in a wonderland peopled with all sorts of fantastic creatures who go through all sorts of amusing antics for her entertainment. When the average woman marries, she, too, falls asleep, so to speak, in a dreamland of love and security provided by her husband. Then, daily in our country, an average of thirteen hundred wives awaken to find they are widows in an awesome wonderland.

No wonder, they wonder. For it, too, is peopled with various protagonists, some of whom must be called upon in many cases to lead them through a maze of legal, financial, and personal perplexities. Nothing in such a situation is amusing to any widow. Some few people are kind-hearted. Most are frankly indifferent. And not a few are black-hearted.

Widows have been rooked, beyond calculation, by almost every kind of crook, from the rifler who swipes and forges a pension check to the smooth swindler who "works" the widows of wealthy men. In the interest of their 240,000 dependent children, as well as for their own sakes, the more than 400,000 women who enter widowhood in an average year must be sagacious in the management of their resources. Every widow may not possess wisdom in matters of money. But every widow may look askance at any financial proposition presented by a relative, friend, or stranger.

Before making any important expenditure or investment, she must seek the advice, appraisal, and approval of impartial, vigilant and capable consultants. Perturbed mentally and distressed physically, particularly during the period of adjustment, to whom may a widow turn for advice and assistance? Instinctively, in her innocence and impairment, she would look to close relatives and intimate friends. But they, too, may be disturbed by her husband's death, and equally dark as regards the best course to pursue.

Obviously, employment of professional experience is essential. But an intruding thought bespeaks caution on the score of relatives and friends in the professions. Even when such persons are ethical and capable, it is not altogether wise to employ them. They may accept nothing or too little for their services. Or, they may manage to take too much. In these eventualities, there is possibility of embarrassment, or obligation, or rancour as a result.

Propriety aside, is it prudent to accept such service, even when it is volunteered? Will the fee-free service rendered by an attorney, a physician, or an investment counselor have substance, or will it be suspect? In any matter involving compensation for service, isn't it better to be impersonal, circumspect, and explicit?

When medical attention, of itself, is not sufficiently effective in affording an afflicted person a measure of ease, it should be supplemented with spiritual alleviation.

A bereaved woman need not stand on ceremony with respect to the physician or the pastor. The one, in administering physical comfort, will ease her mind. The other, in affording mental solace, will often relieve physical distress also. So, it matters not much which is seen first.

Should it be the pastor, naturally and preferably he should be the religious leader of the church in which her family maintains membership, if it has a church affiliation. If he is by training, as well as by talent, the kind of clergyman he should be, he will not wait over-long to make a subsequent call, assuming he did come to her before the service to offer spiritual comfort.

While it may not be within a pastor's province to do so, he may be willing and able to advise a widow concerning various vital matters of a material nature. Many a minister has had broad experience with life and its problems. His contacts with business and professional men may stand her in good stead, for he may be able to direct her to conscientious individuals and institutions capable of dealing with her problems. However, with respect to financial matters, she will seldom err if she is careful to deal with a reputable, friendly banker.

Today, almost without exception, all banks are safe banks. All "national" banks are members of the Federal Reserve System, and are subject to at least twice-a-year inspections. It is mandatory for a national bank to obtain membership in the Federal Deposit Insurance Corporation, which insures individual deposits to the extent of $10,000. State banks are under the scrutiny of the state superintendent of banks. Although the FDIC insurance is optional with state banks, many of them avail themselves of this service.

HOW TO MAKE A VALID WILL

The husband of one widow died intestate—meaning he left no will designating heirs and the disposition to be made of his property. His interests were diversified and extensive. "By the time the estate was settled," laments the widow, "I was a physical and mental wreck, and the delays and extra expenses it took didn't help the situation any. I have no intention of leaving my family with such a burden of legal and financial problems. I want to make a will as soon as possible. How should I go about it?"

The laws state specifically how a person's property is to be distributed when he passes on without leaving a valid will. From her own experience, this lady is already familiar with that fact. She is also now aware that a settlement made according to legal enactments may not cover the circumstances that pertain to a particular family.

Within legal limits, a will provides assurance that a person's property will be distributed as he deems best. The testator can also select the person or persons he would want to discharge that obligation.

Several requirements are essential to making a will effective. It must be written. It must be signed by the testator. It must be witnessed by no fewer than two persons. It is advisable to have the document drawn up by a qualified attorney.

These are some of the steps that should be followed with regard to composing a will:

1. Compile a record of all assets, so the attorney will have information as to property that is owned individually and that which is owned jointly.

2. Check the beneficiary provisions of life insurance policies.

3. Plan the division of the property with utmost care. On that count, seek the aid of an attorney and accept his advice.

4. If the provisions are complicated, have the lawyer draw up a preliminary draft of the will; then, take enough time to examine it carefully.

5. When the will is ready for signature, the attorney should supervise the signing.

6. Keep a copy of the will, and deposit the original with the attorney, the probate court, or in a secure and accessible place.

7. Whenever a vital change occurs in the family, such as a demise or a marriage, or in its economic condition, the will should be checked and changed if necessary.

A will can always be altered, but that must be done correctly. Present provisions should never be marked out, or new ones written in. When as change is indicated, the attorney should draw up a new will, or prepare a proper amendment to the present document.

Not a few people have asked me why so many people seek information on various problems via the press instead of making direct contact with specialists and constituted agencies. It is not difficult to supply an answer. Many people are averse to approaching professionals and authorities without first posting themselves to some extent on the pros and cons of a problem. They want information that will enable them to present their problems intelligently. With that, they want time to think things over before proceeding. So, they enlist the aid of an impartial third party, often anonymously.

MORE ABOUT WILLS

The laws pertaining to the succession of property from a person deceased to those other persons, related and/or unrelated, whom he has designated by will to be his heirs are not only involved, but vary considerably among the states. So voluminous is the literature on the subject of wills, so vast is the store of lore covering cases where no will has been provided, that it is possible to do no more than offer some suggestions concerning the legal conduct of a widow with respect to the existence or non-existence of a will.

Although we outgrow primitive conditions and customs, and degrees of development, it seems that we cannot rid ourselves completely of the superstitious past. We drag it around with us as a snail drags his shell; a rudiment, a vestige of our progress from the lower to the higher forms of life. All superstitions are senseless enough, but one persists that has been and still is the cause of much trouble. It is the belief that if a person makes a will, he will die shortly thereafter.

With all due respect to the deceased, the man who neglected to, or who refused to make a will did not serve the best interests of his survivors. His evasion of duty or his superstitious fear only served the best interests of other interests, increasing the worries of his widow while decreasing the income he intended for his heirs.

A person's will need be nothing more than a short and simple document stating explicitly what disposition should be made of his estate.

In the case of a married man, his will should have named his wife sole executrix without bond, provided she was a competent person. Such an instrument would have permitted her to execute his wishes as expressed in his will. (However, when his assets are of considerable worth, highly diversified and involved, it is advisable to name an experienced executor such as the trust department of a modern bank.) She would not then be required to pay a bonding company to protect the estate against the possibility that she might appropriate any of the property before it becomes legally hers. And it would enable his estate to save a substantial sum that would otherwise go to defray executor's fees.

When a man passes on without leaving a properly designed will in a safe but accessible place, he is said to have died intestate. Therefore, within a reasonable period of time, application must be made to the court having jurisdiction in such matters to have an administrator of the estate appointed. Incidentally, many courts for a small fee provide facilities for the safekeeping of wills.

Most jurisdictions recognize that the widow of the

deceased is a proper and qualified person to fill the office of administrator. She may decline this obligation. Usually, the cost of administering an estate is set by state statute and is based principally on a percentage of the amount involved. Therefore, a widow might feel that she ought to obtain the administrator's fee for herself.

That point gives rise to quite a question in some cases: Should the widow attempt to undertake the prolonged legal procedure involved in the termination of an estate? An affirmative answer depends on several conditions; her personal inclination, her nervous temperament, her practical business ability, and the state of her health. Despondency, as well as any or all of the aforesaid conditions may deter her from assuming the unfamiliar and diverse duties involved in discharging her responsibility. Then it behooves her to shift the burden to someone better able and better qualified to bear it.

A trustworthy near relative, or an intimate family friend equal to the requirement should be chosen to exercise authority in her stead. But it matters not who undertakes the duty; the aid of a capable, conscientious attorney should be secured to set her and keep her, or the person who serves in her stead, on a proper course of procedure. It is wise not to let a matter of this nature become more involved than it would be, as a matter of course.

COMPETENT LAWYER SHOULD SETTLE ESTATE

A man may live the scriptural span of three score years and ten, or longer, without once requiring the services of an attorney. But after his death, the person designated to settle his estate—usually his widow— must of necessity secure the services of legal counsel.

The legal disposition of property after death is an intricate matter and the executor or executrix is obligated to discharge properly the duty which has been imposed by the deceased person. If necessary, selection of legal counsel is a matter that should be undertaken with considerable care. The individual selected must be competent as a counselor and have probity as a person.

Even as every human need nurtures its business or a profession, every calling has its saints and its sinners, its "shysters" in the legal profession. By the very nature of his calling, a person versed in the law can contrive to circumvent the law for personal gain, yet evade the penalty. Such maneuvers, while legally permissible, perhaps, are ethically questionable, and highly deplorable as far as the client is concerned.

Every executrix should exercise extraordinary care in avoiding the so called "friend of the family" who may degenerate rapidly into a person with criminal intent when exposed to an opportunity to "grab some easy money" from an unsuspecting and inexperienced person.

If a widow knows of no lawyer in whom she can

place implicit trust, ways of selecting an experienced, ethical person are herewith suggested:

Certain relatives with considerable business experience should be able to direct her to a suitable attorney. Business associates and close friends of her late husband should be able to do likewise.

She may call upon an attorney who handled her husband's legal affairs in a satisfactory manner. Her minister, family doctor, or officers of the bank her husband dealt with should be able to recommend a person who would handle her legal problems properly.

If she feels utterly helpless in this matter, or has any reluctance about approaching any of the afore-mentioned, she may quite properly apply to the Probate Court of her jurisdiction for aid.

Without violating ethical conduct, the court may give her a list of several lawyers from which to select one to serve her requirements.

From the standpoint of fees charged, there is no such thing as a "cheap" lawyer. Apparently, some attorneys charge less for their services than others; but broadly considered, the average able attorney bases his bill for service rendered on several factors:

The total time devoted to the case, and the value and character of the assets, as well as on the ability of the client to pay. With respect to the final factor, a good lawyer is like a good doctor whose first consideration is not the patient's wealth, but his welfare.

In the matter of settling an estate, the courts entertaining jurisdiction in such proceedings will set the fee of the attorney employed, insisting in some instances upon submission of an itemized statement of the amount of service actually rendered.

If the property consists largely of assets that may be converted quickly into cash, such as securities having a day-to-day value, counsel costs would be comparatively low. But when the property is composed for the most part of real estate holdings and/or complete or partial interest in one or more business enterprises, complications may arise that could require more service and thus a commensurate fee for counsel.

TAX DATA

For Federal Income Tax purposes, the marital status of the individual taxpayer is established as of the final day of the taxable year. The widow of a man who expired before the end of the taxable year is deemed to have been married during the entire year. If she remained a widow until the end of the taxable year, she may file a joint return for herself and her deceased husband. A return of that description will enable her to enjoy the benefit of the exemptions and tax computation of a joint return, just as if the marriage had not been disrupted by death.

Additionally, for the two following taxable years she may be entitled, as a surviving spouse, to the benefits of the income-splitting provision if she can meet these requirements:

1. Her husband must have died during her two preceding taxable years.

2. She must have been entitled to file a joint return with her husband for the year in which he died.

3. She must still be, in fact, the widow of the deceased.

4. She must furnish more than half the cost of maintaining a home which is the principal residence of a child or stepchild for whom she claims an exemption.

The widow may not claim exemption for the decedent, but she computes her tax by including in her return only her income, exemptions and deductions, and uses Tax Schedule II, which gives her the split income benefits. She cannot use Form 1040A.

Generally, a joint return for a widow and her deceased husband should be filed by the widow and the executor or administrator. But the widow may file the joint return provided her taxable year and that of the decedent started on the same day and no executor or administrator was appointed prior to the due date for filing the return.

That also applies if the decedent expired after the close of the taxable year and before the due date for filing a return. The return must be filed by the executor or the administrator if one has been appointed. If it is a joint return, it must be signed by the widow also. If no executor or administrator has been appointed, the widow may sign the joint return in one of these ways:

Ann Smith
Ann Smith (Surviving Spouse)
Ann Smith (Taxpayer and Surviving Spouse)

If a refund is due, a *Form 1310, Statement of Claimant to Refund Due on Behalf of Deceased Taxpayer,* must be executed by the person claiming the refund. The form may be had from the District Director. A copy of the certificate of death must accompany the Form 1310.

When an executor or administrator is later appointed, he may deem it advisable to disaffirm the joint return which was filed by the widow. He has one year from the date of the return to file a separate return for the decedent. The joint return which the widow filed will then be regarded as her separate return.

CLAIMS OF CREDITORS CONTROLLED BY LAW

Almost all of the states, either by statute law or judicial decision, exempt the proceeds of life insurance payable to a stated survivor (including the cash-surrender value of a policy) from the claims of the creditors of the assured.

Moreover, most of the states have enacted a provision freeing all or part of the proceeds of a life policy held by an insurance company from the claims of creditors of the beneficiary where the assured has provided that such proceeds are not to be available to the creditors of the beneficiary. Thus, by making proper provision, the assured may insure his insurance. It is advisable to consult a capable attorney regarding the law of any particular jurisdiction as to the manner of provision that will comply with the requirements of the law.

The idea of credit life insurance is not new, since policies can always be written for borrowers, as in the case of a mortgage protection policy to protect the family against the hazard of facing an indebtedness, should the borrower himself die before it is fully repaid. Now, with respect to credit life insurance to cover the more ordinary current accounts, it seems there is a type of insurance to cover every contingency but that.

However, it is possible to provide such protection by taking out comparatively low cost term insurance for the same reason that fire and automobile insurance is procured. The face value of such a policy is usually a sum estimated to cover an incurred amount of indebtedness during a definite period, and is made payable to the estate of the insured with the provision that it be used to discharge his debts.

In the event of the death of the insured, the amount due a creditor would be honored upon presentation of a properly executed claim. Any amount remaining after satisfying creditors' claims would be paid to a contingent beneficiary, generally the widow.

CHARGE ACCOUNTS

Chances are that all accounts owed by a recently bereaved widow and any children in her care were carried in her husband's name. His personal character, capital assets, and ability to meet payments when due were the security that supported the extension of credit. For the purpose of this discussion, accounts due at the time of his demise may be considered separately and may have payment deferred until his estate is settled. However, his widow may wish or find it necessary to open charge accounts in her own name.

She should realize that she no longer has the income of Mrs. John Smith, the wife, but only that of (Mrs.) Mary Smith, the widow, and she should open her accounts in that name.

Now, *her* character, capital, and capacity must stand behind the credit she may secure. Among credit people, there is continuous argument as to which of those factors should be accorded major consideration.

So, to facilitate matters, it would be well for the widow to seek the first credit extension from a firm which has had experience with the family. The widow should have an interview with the credit manager. He will consider the purpose for which the credit is sought, the amount involved, how repayment may be expected, and from what sources. If the family record is good and its assets are ascertainable, there should be little difficulty in securing the new credit.

The widow whose husband had no established

credit record should expect to experience some delay while her situation is investigated. She, too, should seek an interview with the credit manager of the company from which credit is to be obtained. In her case, the purpose for which credit is sought is considered with great care. If the need is extremely essential, she is more likely to receive favorable consideration.

Perhaps the widow had charge accounts in her maiden name before she married. A record of them, if still available, would be quite helpful. A visit to her local credit bureau might produce the desired information.

A guarantor, some friend of the family perhaps, who will assure the account until the ability of the obligated person becomes established, is another way to secure the initial credit.

Lacking those customary aids, the need for credit and one's personal references assume added importance. If creditable, they are often sufficient to secure the initial extension, after which the paying record of the person obligated will provide the basis for further extension.

Any inability to meet specified terms of payment should be reported immediately to the credit manager, together with reasons why. His advice and counsel should not only be sought, but accepted. He is deeply interested in indicating to troubled debtors how their obligations may be discharged and their credit records maintained.

TANGLED THINKING

In any situation that arouses undue feelings of anxiety, even a modicum of straight thinking is worth more than months of pointless worrying. The foregoing is said with respect to a letter received from a worried widow. A rather long and vague recital of her woes and worries, it is here summarized. Its very nature indicates the lack of purposeful thinking which is necessary to arrive at a successful solution.

She deplored her lot in life generally, mentioned she was suffering from some unspecified disease, stated she was working under a handicap due to her illness, alluded to her precarious financial condition, and regretted that she had no one to look to for advice. Therefore, she was turning to a stranger with apologies for doing so.

It took several studied readings of the letter to come to a fairly concrete conclusion regarding this case. If "money is the root of all evil," it is probably the root from which grows her disease of mind and body. And, according to what she revealed, money should be the least of her troubles. She occupies an apartment with her mother who is able to contribute to the living expenses. Additionally, they have a paying roomer and that helps with the rent. As for other income, she is gainfully employed four days a week.

But, this is the thing that untied the knot in her tangled thinking: She stated, in so many words, that she had $12,000 in a savings account that was earning

2½ per cent interest. As a matter of fact, such companies in her city were paying 3 per cent.

She was thinking of withdrawing this money and putting it into real estate or stocks, hoping that so invested, it would yield enough to make her financially independent. Was that possible, she wanted to know.

Considering the commercial aspects of the case, a direct recommendation cannot be made. Whatever may be offered in the way of advice must be limited to a presentation of facts and figures, with a suggestion that the reader study the information and come to her own conclusions.

The following compilation sets forth the facts comprehensively with a minimum of comment regarding investment possibilities:

Real estate yields from 7 to 10 per cent. On a 100 per cent basis, the cash conversion factor is approximately 60, and the anxiety factor is high.

Common stocks earn from 3½ to 6½ per cent, while the liquidity factor is around 55, and the worry factor is rather high.

Mutual funds return from 3 to 5 per cent; the safety factor being about 65, and the anxiety factor moderate.

Credit unions yield from 2½ to 5 per cent. The cash conversion factor verges upon 100, and the worry factor is nil.

Annuities earn from 2 to 2¾ per cent and are completely safe.

Insured building and loan accounts pay from 2½ to

3½ per cent, with a safety factor close to 100, and no worry factor.

U.S. "E" Bonds (purchased after February 1, 1957, and held to maturity) earn 3¼ per cent and are 100% safe without worry.

Savings banks pay 2 to 3 per cent, are 100% liquid and worry-free.

The $12,000 could be divided several ways for investment in various enterprises to yield 4 per cent, or better. Such management would also yield greater peace of mind despite changing economic conditions.

If she will arrange to invest her money to yield 4 per cent (compounded annually), and if she is able to leave it so until she is 65 and eligible for Social Security, her money will have grown to a figure approximating $29,000.

The life expectancy for women who reach 65 is reported to be 80 years. Her savings and Social Security should supply her with ample support during her remaining years.

WOMEN BUSINESS PARTNERS FACE BREAKUP AFTER DEATH

Elizabeth was not a young woman when she married. In fact, she was middle-aged. Nathan, her husband, had been a widower. He passed away less than two years after their marriage.

She had worked for Nathan and his partner, Roy, for almost twenty years, and inherited her husband's share of the business.

In addition to continuing as the store's bookkeeper-cashier, she assumed certain management responsibilities. Elizabeth and Roy got along well together, and their business made money.

Roy was killed in an auto accident when he was returning home from a buying trip to Cleveland. His widow, Alice, who is about fifteen years younger than Elizabeth, inherited Roy's share of the business.

After a few weeks, Alice decided to take an active part in the business herself, "to look after her interest," as she announced. She and Elizabeth got off on the wrong foot right from the start.

Alice knows nothing of practical worth to any business; yet, without having any sort of understanding with Elizabeth, she assumed activities that are beyond her ability, and an attitude that rankles Elizabeth.

The situation went from bad to worse, and finally reached a point where Elizabeth offered to buy Alice's interest. But Alice will not sell unless she gets "her price"—which is outrageous and bears no relation to sound business principles.

"I am pretty sick of the whole situation," says Elizabeth. "I mean really sick to my soul, and there is no sense in going on this way.

"There is a young clerk working in the store, and they seem to be getting pretty sweet on each other. I have an idea he is putting her up to all this. So there would be more trouble if I wanted to let him go.

"Maybe I've lost my perspective on the whole situation. If you think I have, will you please help me try to see things as I should?"

If what has been revealed regarding Alice's behavior is factual, then Elizabeth would seem to be quite blameless, although her thinking undoubtedly is pretty well tangled up with various emotional turmoils.

As for Elizabeth feeling about Alice as she does, she may merit criticism for the reason that she is a much more mature person in years, in experience, and no doubt, as a result, in intelligence. So, it would seem that Elizabeth's first obligation to herself and to everyone and everything else involved in the situation is to master her own emotions.

It is doubtful if the person lives, or ever has lived who has never felt fear, frustration, and defeat. Those feelings can and must be overcome, and when Elizabeth accomplishes that, she will be able to think more clearly and act more becomingly as a person and as a business woman.

She has a mature mind. She has the intelligence to root out the agitation and the rancour she feels toward Alice. She must use it. Then, if she feels she cannot accept the situation, she must act to resolve it.

If the latter course is to be the case, she will need the offices of a competent third party for purposes of mediation. Her business banker, for instance. His intervention should be invited. The facts should be laid before him. He knows business, and the business in question in particular, and he will know what to say.

Then, if Alice is still contrary and adamant, Elizabeth's most advisable recourse, perhaps, would be to engage a lawyer to start proceedings to resolve the partnership.

First, she should try the peaceful way. It may prevail.

BEWARE OF "BAIT" ADVERTISING

"There are two classes of men, the righteous, who think themselves to be sinners, and the sinners, who think themselves to be righteous." This sage observation was made by Blaise Pascal, a French philosopher, whose death occurred about three hundred years ago. It applies with equal effect today to a type of tradesman who regards himself as an upright businessman when, essentially, he is little better than a downright crook. We refer to the user of "bait" advertising—a device which is used to entice the unwary into buying much higher priced merchandise.

The Federal Trade Commission has denounced "bait" advertising as a menace to the public's pocketbook. It frequently orders firms using such advertising to cease and desist. The FTC notes that many poor people are victims of these hoodwinkers, including oldsters living on modest pensions. It cited the case of a New Jersey widow who was beguiled by the offer of a $29.50 sewing machine.

She persuaded herself that she could pinch out this amount from her $80-a-month pension and eventually pay for it by making her own clothing. Seeing the machine advertised in a local newspaper, she telephoned the store offering it. A salesman came to her home without a "bargain" machine. He stated that the store was out of them temporarily, but he requested and received a deposit of $10. Several days later, the salesman brought her the advertised machine. The widow tried to sew on it, but she testified that she couldn't use it because it "jumped all over the table."

The salesman, of course, had another machine with him for $169 and the down payment would, by happy coincidence, amount to just $29.50. Cheap at the price, too, he confided, because there was a scratch on it. Bewildered, the widow paid the remaining $19.50. The ensuing payments were too much for her and the machine was repossessed. There was no refund of the amounts she had paid, and no homemade clothing to comfort her in the future. "Bait" advertising had deluded another victim.

The Federal Trade Commission states that "bait" advertising cannot be identified by any single sign of evil intent. It takes a combination of factors to put a prospect on guard.

These are the stop signs to watch for:

1. A product priced at a startlingly lower price than that charged for the same kind of product at other stores.

2. Reluctance on the part of the salesman to show the advertised product.

3. Disparagement of the advertised product, and insistence by the salesman on showing more expensive types.

4. Explanation that the advertised product on hand is only a floor sample and that long delay will be encountered in getting others like it.

5. A sell-out of the "bargain" in a suspiciously short time, "but let me show you something else even better."

To which we add: "Walk with the wise, and be wise."

GOOD RECORD KEEPING SYSTEM IMPORTANT IN "FAMILY" STORE

"When my husband passed away two years ago, I decided to keep the store and run it myself with the help of the children. It is a general store in a small town. We have two small factories and a good trade territory. I had a buyer, but I decided it would be better for me to keep the store.

"I always helped my husband in the store when I could. I knew the business, and I knew I would have to keep myself busy to keep from thinking too much about the past. Also, the store, while it never made a lot of money, made us a fair living, and I still had two growing children on my hands to support. I thought with their help I could manage the store, so I kept it, but it isn't working out as I hoped.

"I am in financial trouble already, and I can't seem to put my finger on what is wrong. We try to hold expenses down by taking only what we need to live. People are still trading with us like always, and we seem to be doing as much business as before. Maybe you can give me an idea."

The lady who wrote that letter thanked me in advance, and signed her name. She stated that she couldn't seem to put her finger on what was ailing her store. But I was quite sure I could put my finger on the sore spot before I finished reading her letter. There seemed to be a "mouse in the meal," so to speak. In fact, several mischief makers.

A number of things could have gone amiss. Since the business had been financially sound under her husband's management, and sales volume had not decreased, it seems fair to assume that the store's record-keeping system, simple as it would be, has been permitted to go to pot.

The reason so many stores face failure and eventually become bankrupt is this: No records at all are kept, or if any are kept, they are faulty. That is particularly the case with so many "mama-papa" and "family" stores.

And the most common factor contributing to that condition is this: Mixing the family expenses with the store expenses and neglecting to keep accurate record of both the cash and the merchandise that is needed and taken for personal and family use.

Evidently, her husband kept track of these withdrawals, at least to an extent. Evidently, she does not. In many stores where such practices are permitted, it is next to impossible to know what the store is doing.

To remedy such a situation, if it has been diagnosed correctly, this woman and her children must adjust their out-go to their income. The first thing she should do is to determine a weekly wage for herself, and then allowances for her children. They all work in the store. They are all entitled to receive fair and logical earnings, and those earnings are legitimate business expenses chargeable to overhead.

Those wages should be based on what the business can afford to pay, not on what the retailer thinks she and her children ought to have. Then, they must adjust their living expenses to their wages. That means that each week, each one should receive his wages just as if he were an employee of the store. When they "buy" merchandise from themselves, it should be done on a business basis, just as if they were customers. Preferably, they should pay cash, but if they "charge it," the account should be settled every week.

All this situation seems to need is a little common sense and a lot of self-restraint. Both are worth their weight in dollars.

PROPER USE OF CREDIT AIDS OPERATION OF SMALL BUSINESS

"Some time ago, I read an article of yours which explained to a widow that mixing up her own family expense with her business expenses is what may have caused her to get into financial trouble.

"I, too, am a widow, and I am thinking seriously of taking over a little business. It is a small gift shop in a good suburban neighborhood. If I pay cash for the shop, I won't have too much working capital. For a while, at least, and until I can build up the business, I will need to ask for credit. How would I go about doing that?"

Most retail merchants do the bulk of their buying on a credit basis. The advantages of credit buying are significant. To be specific: It is more convenient because it allows more time to check invoices. All of one week's or one month's bills may be gathered together and paid at one time.

It does away with C.O.D. deliveries which may arrive at times when it may not be convenient to make payment.

The amount of credit extended by a supplier is actually an addition to the merchant's working capital.

Since credit is an asset of vital value, the retailer should understand how to get it and how to keep it.

To obtain a line of credit, it is first necessary to give the supplier assurance that he will not lose money by charging goods to you. You must be able to convince him that you are able and willing to pay his bills when they fall due. Your ability to do that will depend mainly on how well you operate your store.

If you run it well enough to make a proper profit, it is quite likely that you will be able to pay your bills on time. You can offer no better proof than a profit-and-loss statement showing that you are running a profitable business.

The wholesaler will want to know that you are not already overburdened with obligations. He will not accept estimates or guesses. He will want to know exactly what you may owe and to whom.

Don't think that that is none of the supplier's business. It is his business most assuredly for the reason that the soundness of his own business depends on keeping the risk he must assume within reasonable limits. The supplier who can serve you best with respect to goods, service, and prices is the very one who will insist on having evidence of your ability to pay.

There is a certain distinction between the company that supplies goods on consignment and the traditional supplier. The consignment house does not extend credit, as such, for the reason that it retains title to the goods and the sales until remittances for goods sold have been received. Nevertheless, the consignee must give assurance that he is credit-worthy and morally upright in order to be entrusted with an amount of working capital in the form and value of the goods consigned.

Some merchants object to giving a supplier the information required for credit purposes. Some don't because they can't. If you can, give the facts promptly and completely. You will improve your standing immediately.

After you have secured a credit standing, make

every effort to maintain and increase it. One way to do that is to become a desirable customer; a good customer. A good customer buys a reasonable amount of goods and pays his invoices promptly when due.

Of course, you should always do some shopping around in your own interest, but you will not build a substantial standing with any one or two suppliers by buying from a dozen competitors. Give as much of your business as possible to a few good houses. Those houses then will take a greater interest in you, and they will be more willing to carry you through a tight place if you ever find yourself in one.

Pay your bills on time and take the cash discount to which you are entitled. But if you are not entitled to it, don't take it.

Occasionally and reluctantly, a supplier will allow an unearned discount to be taken. If such a practice becomes a habit, you will hurt your good will with the supplier.

Even if your store is small, you will become a good credit risk and a good customer by conducting your business in a businesslike way, in every way.

INHERITANCE TAXES

Most of us are familiar with the expression "Just as sure as death and taxes."

Theresa, a widow I have known for many years, is only too familiar with the "death" part of the quotation; but she is not so sure about the "taxes" part.

About three years ago, she and two other relatives inherited her father's estate. Now she wants to know if it is too late for them to claim a federal income tax refund for what she regards as the inheritance taxes they have since paid.

It required a good deal of questioning on my part to clarify the situation. In the process, I learned that they did not inherit the estate, but that her father had set up a trust from which they receive part of the proceeds.

Any federal inheritance taxes that were involved were paid by the executor. Theresa and her relatives are required to pay income tax on the part of the proceeds each receives.

SOCIAL SECURITY

"Honestly, Mr. Zalk, I get sick to my soul every time my son-in-law starts to rant and rave about Social Security—which is just about every payday.

"He earns $100 a week and seldom fails to take the check stub and show my daughter the $2.25 that is held out for Social Security. He says it's nothing but government graft, pure and simple, and that the benefits don't amount to a 'hill of beans' if anyone gets anything.

"I am a widow who has to work because I was left with very little insurance and am not entitled to Social Security. It would have been a very wonderful thing for me and my children if we had survivors' insurance.

"I don't like to hear him carry on like that. What can I say to him to shut him up once and for all?"

Keeping in mind that a "man convinced against his will is of the same opinion still," it might be possible to squelch him with these authentic facts and figures: At the end of 1955, more than 290,000 widows under 65 with dependent children, and more than a million children were receiving survivor benefits based on the Social Security accounts of their deceased husbands or fathers. Among these survivor families, a widowed mother with two children averaged a monthly benefit of $135. Approximately 17 per cent of all the beneficiaries were young children.

If this widow's son should pass on, and if his family would be entitled to the average monthly benefit, his annual Social Security payment at the current rate would amount to less than each monthly payment his family might receive.

A number of important questions put to me by my readers in several states were answered by mail. The answers are here repeated for the information of any and all readers of this volume.

In all states, the husband and father primarily is responsible for family support. If the father is dead the duty devolves upon the mother.

Regarding disposition of property after death, married women may dispose of their separate property by will as freely as married men.

Two of the community-property states, Nevada and New Mexico, limit a wife's testamentary rights to her half of the community estate.

In the absence of a will, a widow (or widower) inherits similar portions from the deceased spouse in most states.

Practically all the states require maintenance for the widow from the husband's estate during the settlement period.

Mrs. J. A. S. has been widowed twice. Her first husband passed away when she was 61; the second, when she was 64, after two years of marriage. Both men had Social Security accounts, but that of the first would provide the widow with larger monthly payments.

She will soon apply for benefits, and wants to know if her payments will be based on the account of her first spouse, or on that of the second.

The philosophy of Social Security is that it replaces the economic loss sustained by eligible survivors, at least to an extent. Prior to the 1956 amendments to the Social Security law, when a widow remarried and there were no dependent, natural, or adopted children, she forfeited all claim to benefits from the account of her former husband. That was because she secured a subsequent means of support. Furthermore, she secured no benefits from the account of her second husband if he died within a year of their remarriage and there were no children.

That provision was to deter women whose main interest in entering into marriage was to secure the Social Security benefits which might come to them as the result of such a union.

Starting with November 1956, if the second husband dies within a year of her remarriage and there are no dependent, natural, or adopted children, the law reestablishes a widow's rights in the account of her former husband.

As I see it, Mrs. S. would not be entitled to receive the larger payments for the reason that her second spouse died after the first year of her remarriage.

CHAPTER IV

CARE OF CHILDREN

IMPORTANCE OF CHILD TRAINING

Widows and orphans! From days of yore to yester-
day and today, so it has ever been and so it will ever
be through all the tomorrows. Some widowhood and
some orphanhood in the population is inevitable, for
while male mortality at all ages may be reduced, it
can never be eliminated.

Indeed, Nature seems to work in mysterious ways
her wonders to perform. Obviously, some natural law
weighs in favor of survival of the mother in the vast
majority of families broken by death—for "a fatherless
child is half an orphan, a motherless child a whole
one."

There is one thing the widowed mother must always remember and never forget: the inadvisability
of over-indulging a child, in any way, to compensate

for the loss of the father. In that, there are two risky possibilities.

For one thing, she may deplete her resources, physical as well as financial. For another, undue compassion, concessions, and compliances may make the child so dependent on her that he will be deprived of the priceless opportunity of becoming largely self-sufficient and self-reliant. No widow, and no orphan of understanding age, can afford to toy with that thought. No parental ambition exceeds the desire to see a child pass successfully from one stage of life to another—from budding childhood to an adulthood in which the highest of human possibilities are attained.

To train and to restrain a child properly is the paramount duty of every widowed mother—for to a large extent, she will have to fulfill the functions of a father as well as a mother in the lives of her children. All the advantages of good character may be obtained for a child whose mother is sincerely interested in instilling in the child ideas that make for satisfactory and successful living.

Each child should be studied. His capabilities should be considered. His present attainments should be appraised. A development program should be planned, one that is not necessarily obvious to the child. And it should not be onerous lest it defeat its purpose. The mother should encourage every good trait in the child and endeavor to eradicate through precept and example every undesirable peculiarity. Some children possess less power of perception than others. With them, patience must be practiced. What they lack in natural ability, they may supply in tractability.

In all activities that can be shared, the mother should be a companion to the child, but she should not dominate him. Conversation should be encouraged. They should talk together freely and frequently. When he is accorded a listening ear, he will reveal his interests and innermost feelings, and indicate which way the wind blows. The child should be taught to think for himself, to use his own judgement, to become self-reliant. His abilities should be tested tactfully and constantly and, as warranted, more and more responsibility should be delegated to him.

Reasonable insistence should be placed upon prompt and willing obedience. If necessary, the reasons for making certain requests should be given, but the consequences of disobedience should not be discussed. That could result in disputes and in a disposition to disobey.

Vital above all else is the necessity of keeping a child valuably occupied; to keep him thinking along clean and constructive lines; to help him avoid companions and environments that are without virtue.

However, the personal conduct of the parent or guardian is usually the prevailing influence in a child's life, and it exerts its most effective power during his early years. This imposes an enormous responsibility on mothers who become widows during their midlife or younger years. It is they who will have to mother-father approximately a quarter of a million children who become orphans in an average year.

Setting a good example in every respect, at least to the extent possible, is a debit which is due every orphan. When the books are balanced, it will be an important item to a mother's credit in any accounting that sums up her effort to guide the mental and moral development of a child.

LAGGARD CHILDREN

A laggard lad or lass is generally a "troublesome" child for any mother. For a widowed mother who has the double duty of rearing and at the same time working to support a family, such a child is a distressing bit of humanity. As one mother told me: "Donald gives me a case of nervous prostration almost every morning of the school week. But on Saturdays, Sundays, and holidays, you'd never know he was the same boy. I don't know what to do about him."

Don is an adolescent. Most dawdling children are in the early youth and adolescent stages of development, 12 through 14 and 15 through 18 respectively. Such children pose a somewhat difficult, but not a hopeless problem.

The trouble may be traced to impaired health, or to some aversion which has been acquired or imposed. Frequently, it will be found in the fact that the child lacks self-reliance. Nagging, threatening, and scolding will not effect relief or a cure. By making the child resentful and deaf to reason, such measures may contribute to aggravating the trouble. If a medical checkup by a doctor indicates no illness in the child that would induce laziness or loitering, the mother should look to the child's study, sleeping, dressing, eating, and toilet habits.

Does he go to bed on time so that he will arise on time, rested and ready for the new day?

Does he sleep serenely or fitfully? Is he disturbed by noises, or by another person occupying the same bed or the same room? Is the bedroom well ventilated, or so stuffy that the child is too dopey to bestir himself upon awakening?

Are his school supplies and clothing made ready before he retires so that he can start the new day without difficulty and delay?

Does he eat with evident enjoyment the food that is served to him, or does he dilly-dally over almost every dish? There is virtue in taking enough time to eat properly, but undue delay cannot be considered commendable.

Is he obliged to stay up late to complete his homework assignments because he frittered away the earlier hours in activities of smaller importance?

Does he tarry unduly on the toilet because of delayed evacuation? Constipation is a condition which can and should be corrected for reasons of present and future well-being.

Does the cosmetic-conscious teen-age girl spend more time of a morning than is mete in applying her makeup? She certainly can have a time-consuming time of it with a lipstick and adventures in its application.

If any one or any combination of these considerations cannot be held responsible for a child's procrastination in getting off to school promptly, then the mother should probe sources outside the home for the core of the problem.

Is the child trying to avoid attendance at school because his homework is often neglected? Or because he thinks he is in disfavor with a teacher? Or because some neighborhood bully frightens him on his way to and from school? Or because he is shunned by his schoolmates for some childish or serious reason?

Any of these common causes of school-morning-slowness may be basically an attempt to avoid an apprehension of some sort.

To "train up a child in the way he should go" is the prime responsibility of motherhood. Any mother who has deferred this duty for any reason within her control, cannot blame the child for her present plight. Her best recourse is to try to remedy the situation by undertaking a program to correct the child in things in which he is remiss—and to carry it through with patience and consummate tact.

DEPENDENCY OF ORPHANS

Children, as a group, constitute the most needy, the most dependent segment of any population. The neediest children of all are usually found in fatherless families because they have been deprived of the support usually provided by the principal bread-winner.

The vast majority of dependent children, about 90 per cent, is found in husband-wife families; in "normal" families. The second largest number of dependent children, approximately 9 per cent, is found in families headed by widows; in broken families.

Adequacy of family income is directly related to the number of persons who share it.

Studies by several government agencies reveal two significant facts: (1) The least favorable distribution of income is in families headed by widows. (2) The more persons per family, the less income per capita.

These facts may be dramatically demonstrated with an example consisting of a 4-person family that must live entirely (or to a large extent) on monthly Social Security payments.

Number of Persons in Family	Monthly Soc. Sec. Payment	Average Per Person
1 Person (Widow alone)	$75.40	$75.40
2 Persons (Widow and one child)	$150.80	$75.40
3 Persons (Widow and two children)	$200.00	$66.65
4 Persons (Widow and three children)	$200.00	$50.00

Obviously, a widow so situated must manage on that; with what has been saved, if anything, and with what she may be able to obtain from other sources. The more persons she must shelter, the more mouths she must feed, the more bodies she must clothe, the more prudently she must manage. That calls for action. And not delayed action.

First: She must explore her entire income potential, that part which is positive as well as that which is tentative.

Second: She must then plan a budget on a sound foundation of facts, which omits every mite of wishful thinking.

She must plan her own manner of living within the limits of an assured amount of income, and then live her own plan.

The only useful suggestions that anyone may venture in the matter of budget planning must be based on broad general experience and on accepted data regarding the three basic requirements: Food, clothing, and shelter.

PLAN NOURISHING MEALS

We all know how it is with meals. When Dad could not come home to dinner, a light lunch was usually substituted for the substantial noonday or evening meal. Now that Dad can never come home again, what will the practice be? Will the children continue to be fed from bottles, bags, and boxes? Not for long, and not often if their health is to be maintained.

When the regular pay checks that provided plenty of necessary, nourishing food are no longer forthcoming, mother must plan her meal-making as she never planned before. Teen-age children need as much nourishing food as an adult. Often more. For building strong, healthy bodies, younger children need the same kind of food, but more simply prepared.

In a booklet on food for the family with young children, published by the Federal Government, there is a schedule which suggests a healthful diet for a family of four at a cost of $17 to $19 a week, based on prevailing prices as of March 1955.

For a moderately active, widowed mother with one teen-age and two pre- or primary school children, food would cost about $960 a year, or approximately 40 per cent of an annual income of $2400.

The schedule does not provide for much variety, but with careful planning and preparation, the food should prove quite enjoyable. This is the schedule according to the "Basic 7" National Food Guide:

Leafy, green, and yellow vegetables 8 to 9 lbs.
Citrus fruit, tomatoes .... 7 to 8 lbs.
Potatoes, sweet potatoes .... 9 to 10 lbs.
Other vegetables and fruits ...... 6 to 7 lbs.
Milk .... 17 quarts
Meat, poultry, fish .... 5 to 6 lbs.
Eggs .... 1⅔ doz.
Dry beans, peas, nuts .... ¾ to 1 lb.
Flour, cereals, meal .... 10 to 11 lbs.
Fats, oils .... 2 to 2½ lbs.
Sugar, syrup, preserves .... 2 to 2½ lbs.

To provide such a good, inexpensive diet, the mother will have to plan and to shop with considerable care, even though some of the cheaper items are high in food value.

Aimless shopping must be avoided. Planning should be done in the home, not in the store. Every weekly grocery list should take careful account of what is actually needed to supplement what is on hand. That is the way to avoid overstocking and over-spending. That is one important factor in keeping the family's money problems at a minimum.

BUDGET ESSENTIALS

It is much more difficult to establish a minimum standard for clothing than it is for food. Mainly, this is due to the fact that there is little to show at what point a reduced expenditure for clothing begins to endanger health. Beyond the point of providing certain essentials of covering for the body, clothing standards become affected by personal inclinations and social pressures. "The fashion doth wear out more apparel than the man," said Shakespeare in one of his plays.

Various studies have been made, however, to determine a standard for a minimum clothing expenditure that will maintain a proper or passable appearance and provide healthful covering for the body. For that purpose, authorities allot about 12 per cent of the

total annual income. Applied to an annual income of
$2400, it amounts to $288.

Admittedly, that is a small amount of money to
cover the cost of even essential clothing needs, but it
spells financial safety for the families concerned.

On the basis of the studies made, the following
schedule has been contrived to chart annual clothing
costs for a mother with three dependent children.
(Average monthly allowance for each person will be
obtained by dividing the annual figure by 12.)

Mother	$92
Boy or girl (14-17)	92
Child (9-13)	62
Child (under 9)	42
Total	$288

Thus far, more than half, specifically $1248 of the
$2400 annual income, has been allocated to food and
clothing. So now rent, the third major item in the
family budget, must come in for consideration.

Based on average contract rent for tenant-occupied
dwellings, and on the average estimated rental value
of owner-occupied homes, it appears that approximately 30 per cent of the annual income will be required for rent.

With respect to the "sample" family under consideration, the rent requirement would be about $720
a year.

So, we have worked our way through words and

figures to the point where it looks like 82 per cent of the $2400, or $1968 will be needed for food, clothing and shelter—which will leave 18 per cent, or $242 for everything else.

Evidently, it is now time to give thought to how the complete budget plan might look. This is suggested:

Food	$960
Clothing	288
Shelter	720
Operating	168
Savings	120
Miscellaneous	144

Confronted with the complicated problem of planning a budget, there wells up in us a fraternal feeling for the "dodo" in the story of *Alice in Wonderland*. We recall that when he tried with difficulty to explain the running of a "caucus" race, he crawled out of it by saying: "The best way to explain it is to do it."

Leah, now a widow, mothered two sons. The younger, Jay, honored his father and his mother. He was killed in action in World War II. Her husband, hard hit by the boy's death, became despondent. His health declined, and he died a few years later.

The older son, Martin, also saw military service. He returned unscathed physically and unchanged mentally. Always something of a problem child, he gave no comfort to his father or to his mother. His continued misbehavior in manhood drove his father into a deeper state of dejection.

When Martin was released from military service, he was given a place and an interest in his father's retail business. However, his main interest was not in merchandising, but in gambling. In particular on horse races.

A rabid and unrealistic bettor, Martin lost consistently and considerably. Whenever the ponies threw him for a sizable loss, the cash register had to pony up reimbursement. When the cashier protested, his father would say, "Balance your books, and I'll make up the difference from my own pocket."

After her husband's death, Leah had to contend with the same thing. And more.

As part owner of the store, Martin liked to throw his weight around. He became so obnoxious that the store's capable manager and several skillful salesmen quit and went to work for competitors. They had a following of customers who went with them. That hurt the business; not seriously, but it hurt.

Martin assumed management and made a mess of the entire operation.

He married a good girl, then got mixed up with one not so good. That lost him his wife and cost him plenty. His mother pulled him through that mess.

I was in the store one day making some personal purchases when Leah approached me. "I would like to talk with you if you can spare a little time," she said uneasily. "I have to talk with someone about——well, I'll tell you in the office. I'm a widow with a headache. A big one."

In the office, she told me the whole story; spared no detail, and then stopped, her chin cupped in the question mark formed by her hand and forearm.

"I presume you are looking for a remedy," I remarked.

"A cure would be better," she replied.

"Obviously," I agreed. "Have you ever heard the quotation, 'Diseases desperate grown by desperate appliances are relieved, or not at all?' "

"Seems to me I have; I'm not sure," she hedged.

"Be that as it may, that's the course I would follow," I suggested. "Find a buyer, sell the business, and be done with it and with worrying about an irresponsible son. That could be the making of him."

When I was leaving, Leah said she would think it over. Evidently she did—for a long time. About three years later she sold the business for what it was worth and devoted herself to certain charitable endeavors in the community.

As for Martin, discreet inquiries disclosed that he took his proceeds, opened a shop of his own in a large suburban shopping center, and was making a go of it.

Is it "important" for a girl to have a college education? A widowed mother of two children—twins— Claude, a son, and Claudia, a daughter, wants to know. Both children want to go to college, and their mother wants them to. But they are confronted with a sharp curtailment of funds. The family is still receiving mother's and children's Social Security payments. That income supplemented with permissible earnings enables them to manage quite well.

But soon they will no longer be entitled to receive Social Security benefits, because the children will be over 18 and the mother will be under 62.

It will cost about $2400 a year to give both children a college education and that seems to be out of the question, considering the limited earning capacity of the mother and the children. Working together, they might manage to put one child through college. But which one should have the opportunity? Claude or Claudia?

Implicated as she is in the situation, in a "mother-father" position, the widow wants to maintain strict impartiality with respect to the children. Claudia is all agog about being a career woman. Claude is eager to be an electronics engineer. Their mother is in a dilemma.

The ideas of a person not directly implicated in the situation might be valuable, and these are mine for what they are worth: All things being equal, it would seem that Claude, in this particular case, should have the opportunity to go to college.

While for certain substantial reasons it may be considered "important" for a girl to go to college, it would be imperative for a boy who intends to enter one of the professions as a means of earning an adequate living when he becomes a family man. Since Claudia may marry sooner or later and become occupied with the truly important career of running a home and raising a family, a college education—while desirable and useful—would not be essential for her.

Recent, reliable surveys lend strong support to the foregoing statement. The Woman's Bureau of the U.S. Department of Labor asked several thousand college women about themselves. Four out of five were working in fields for which they had been trained. But only a minority said they were interested in a career. Almost half of them said they considered their employment as only a temporary activity between school and marriage.

Another study of several thousand girls who were selected at random and interviewed by the Institute of Social Research, University of Michigan, showed that "the average American girl is willing to yield personal ambitions for the sake of marriage and motherhood."

For girls, career goals seem to be short-term affairs; for boys, a career is a long-term—in fact, a life-time consideration.

A previous discussion tried to allay the anxiety of a widow whose son thought he couldn't obtain the kind of an education he wanted for the $5000 of insurance money his father had provided for the purpose. With facts and figures, and a few grains of wisdom, I pointed out how the boy could secure a good education, even though he thought he couldn't afford to attend a certain "good" school he had in mind.

In due course, I received a letter from another widow stating that she had scant sympathy for people like the aforementioned mother and son. Her own two sons would be happy to be able to attend even the least expensive school if they could. But they have to work to support themselves and her. They have neither the means nor the time to go to college. She did not ask for any ideas that might possibly help her sons secure an advanced education. Still, there seemed to be an implication in her letter that any suggestions offered would be welcome.

The same mail that brought her letter, brought a note from a friendly reader. A clipping was attached to the note which said: "Perhaps you can use this for your column some time. It's about self-made men. The sons of many widows are just that, you know."

The clipping told the story of two boys. More than 40 years ago, they had started out together as sales clerks for the Lindke Shoe Store in Detroit, Michigan. One sunk his roots in familiar ground in the Detroit area, and attained a sturdy success. The other migrated to Canada, planted himself firmly in its friendly soil and attained similar success. Those boys, now men, were ambitious. They aimed for success with natural aptitudes and acquired skills and scored exceedingly well. They cultivated a true feeling for fine footwear, and genuine respect for their employers and the people they served. They recognized the value of modern merchandising methods and observed the principles of sound management. They applied themselves diligently to self-education. As they gained knowledge, they gained self-respect and the increased regard of others.

Eventually, they were accorded singular honors, as well as business success. Stephen J. Jay became president of the National Shoe Retailers in the United States, and L. H. Wynkie was chosen president of the Canadian Shoe Retailers in Canada.

With the multitude of opportunities for work and self-improvement available to young people today, the trials and tribulations endured by the self-made men of yesteryear seem almost incredible. What they achieved is therefore all the more to their credit and something for others to emulate.

Opportunity knows no limits when one has the will to win. An open, intromittent mind and a stout heart are often more valuable than a big bankroll. It would be well for the impatient to realize that when they cannot push the branches of their progress upward and outward, they can sink the roots of success deeper into richer soil—to sustain and stabilize the success that will come forth in good season.

"I am a working widow—what some people call an employed homemaker," notes Mrs. Edwina H. "I have to work to support my three children and myself. I have been doing that for six years and most of the time I manage to get by.

"I suppose that makes me a successful widow, but I

could be a lot more successful if I would be paid what I was worth. By that I mean I ought to get the same wages a man gets for doing the same kind of work. Honestly, I am doing a better job for less pay than some of the men where I work. I don't loaf and I never lay off, which is more than I can say for some of them.

"To show you what I mean, there is a married man in my department who is doing exactly the same kind of work that I do. He gets about 30 per cent more pay than I do, and he doesn't put himself out. He has only one child to support while I have three. His wife works, too, which I am only mentioning. In other words, I support four myself while he supports three with the help of his wife.

"When I go shopping, the prices are the same for everyone, regardless whether you are a man or a woman, or a wife or a widow. I wonder if my boss ever thinks of that. I see that a lot of the local stores sell what we make and the price is the same everywhere. That means that he has a one-price policy. So why doesn't he pay his women workers the same wages he pays his men for doing the same kind of work?"

It appears that Mrs. H. has made a pretty logical plea for equal-pay legislation which, as yet, has not been enacted in her state and others.

Michigan and Montana, pioneering in equal-pay legislation, enacted the first of such laws in the United States. As of August 15, 1955, sixteen states and Alaska had equal-pay legislation in effect.

The spreading popularity of the equal-pay principle reflects the fact that some 20 million women workers are an important part of the labor force.

Almost one-fourth of all the mothers in the population, with children under 18 years of age, were working in 1952.

In view of the dual duty and the physical strain affecting mothers who are employed outside of their homes, it may be assumed that the vast majority of working mothers are impelled by economic reasons. That explains, to an extent, the enormous difference in the proportion of working mothers who live with their husbands, about 24 per cent, as compared with women who are for the most part widowed, about 53 per cent.

Equal pay protects the wage levels of all workers. It stimulates our national economy by increasing consumer purchasing power. It protects considerate employers from the unfair competition of those who use women to undercut men's wages. It provides greater economic security for working mothers and their dependent children, for it protects the wages of male as well as female heads of families.

Equal pay is a matter of simple justice. It provides equivalent wages for equivalent work, regardless of sex.

Sow the wind and reap the whirlwind. Juvenile delinquency is flying on the wings of a furious wind to become America's No. 1 social scourge.

It is estimated that currently the police come in contact with about a million boys and girls annually on charges of juvenile delinquency. Even if the rate of delinquency does not rise, there is good reason to think that by 1960, the number of juvenile delinquents will increase by 50 per cent.

Children need the stabilizing influence of a satisfactory, normal home life. Denied that, they may easily become delinquent. Society can look to the families disrupted by death and divorce to produce children who are antisocial in many respects. The children of broken families generally continue to reside with their mothers, and just about 80 per cent of those who are under 18 are in the families of widows.

Many of these children start out in life socially or economically handicapped. They feel that they have been treated unfairly, become distrustful and resentful, and are forced to vent their feelings by indulging in anti-social acts of various forms and degrees.

The best way to prevent much present and future juvenile delinquency is to eliminate the bad home and community conditions that breed bad behavior. Thus, children will be made practically immune to becoming involved in serious trouble.

The roots of each human life sink deep and extend far in every direction. When they grow in healthy, enriched earth, the roots will produce sound, healthy plants. In neglected, barren soil, they wither and become weak, and produce plants that are infirm and unpleasing.

In 1950, the Midcentury White House Conference on Children and Youth met in Washington for the commendable purpose of considering what could be done to provide children with the opportunity to grow up as good citizens. From all parts of America, the recognized experts on child development came to that conference, the purpose of which was: "To consider how we can develop in children the mental, emotional, and spiritual qualities essential to individual happiness and to responsible citizenship, and what physical, economic, and social considerations are deemed necessary to this development."

The specific recommendations made by the fact-finding groups and by the Conference with respect to that stated purpose are too extensive to be encompassed within the confines of this chapter. But the recommendations are here summarized in the form of a number of broad objectives which those concerned—parents and organizations—can observe and work upon:

1. Permit no family or child to suffer due to lack of economic security.

2. Help parents to understand and provide better care for their children.

3. See to it that children are not reared in slums and in crowded, impoverished, substandard homes.

4. Provide capable teachers and planned school programs that are capable of catering to the individual needs of children.

5. Provide children with plenty of space in which to play, supplemented by recreational programs that will guide them in making good use of their leisure time.

6. Provide health services that will help children before they become seriously ill; that will maintain their health, and improve their mental and physical powers as well as their personalities.

7. Teach children to live according to an accepted, but reasonable, moral code, so that their relationships with other people will be useful, helpful, and honest.

8. Protect children from any and all influences in the community that might tend to, or try to exploit and corrupt them.

Perhaps not every means by which life can be made better for children has been enumerated here. But those that are listed are vital. They offer the most practical way of preventing the majority of children from becoming delinquent.

ALLOWANCES FOR CHILDREN

"How much spending money should my children have?" asks a widow who was left with a teen-age son and two sub-teen daughters after 14 years of marriage. Her income consists of certain Social Security benefits to which a mother with dependent children is entitled, modest payments from her husband's life insurance, and her earnings from part-time employment—all told, about $360 a month.

"I manage well enough," she admits, but adds: "However, I will not always have what I now have to go on, and I am trying to save every cent I can without begrudging my children spending money." For many widowed mothers, the matter of proper allowances for their children may pose a problem. Yet, it may be worked out easily enough when certain common-sense considerations are employed:

1. How much of the total monthly income may be used to cover realistic allowance requirements for all the children in the family?

2. How much of the total allowance money should be allotted to each child?

3. Will the allowance for each child permit him to make some expenditures for personal purchases and also to save some money?

Every child in the primary school stage of childhood (5½-8 years) should have money of his own to manage, provided he is made to realize that he must pay for certain needs and wants out of his allowance.

Even a pre-school child (3-5½ years) should have money for Sunday School contributions and perhaps for confections.

As children advance in age, their allowances should be increased proportionately to permit purchases of inexpensive personal merchandise. Actual grade school boys and girls (8-11) should begin to develop the habit of saving—thus thriftiness.

Junior high and high school children (12-14) should be expected to buy some of their clothes out of their allowances.

Ideas in infinite variety work incessantly to influence the expenditures of each child as an individual, and each family as a social and economic unit. That is why it is impractical and impossible to say that Bob's allowance should be so much, Bab's so much, and Bea's so much. The proper way to determine a proper allowance for each child is for the family members to get together and arrive at a common understanding. After the family's income has been taken into account, the particular needs of each child should be evaluated. Then, a definite allowance should be granted with agreement as to how the money is to be used.

After an allowance starts, it should be paid regularly. Only in the case of unusual circumstances should there be additional grants. Free-handed giving will destroy the basic idea of granting an allowance which is to instill in each child an increasing sense of financial responsibility. For the same reason, a child's allowance should not be withheld as a means of punishment.

FINANCIAL PROBLEMS GROW

The day a youngster receives his first allowance is the day he starts to have personal financial problems.

Year by year, as he grows older, his situation may become more stringent, especially if he is a member of a fatherless family with limited income. While money management may be only a dime-size problem for a child of primary school age, it may develop gradually to dollar dimension by the time he reaches junior high.

Those statements are supported by a study of junior high and high school students. Dr. Martin Bloom of Springfield, Massachusetts, who conducted the survey, singled out 10th-grade pupils—high school sophomores —as being most concerned with the numerous problems rooted in the need for money.

No matter what these youngsters have in the way of money, it always seems to be little enough. They can always use more to satisfy personal desires and to meet the free-spending competition of fellow students who have plenty and to spare. They would like to have more liberal allowances, or money from part-time jobs. And they wonder if any of their earnings should be given to the family to supplement its income, and why parents feel they should have some control over a child's spending.

Grade 10 seems to be where adolescents arrive at the turning point in their trek to financial freedom, and results in their being afflicted with agitations of one kind or another. Students below and beyond the 10th grade have money problems also, but with less apparent agitation.

Seventh graders concerned about allowances, concentrate on knowing whom to tap, and when.

Eighth graders indicate an important interest in three things: lunch money, how to distribute spending money properly, and having less parental restriction with respect to expenditures.

Getting a job for the purpose of earning some money is a prime concern of the 9th graders; that and becoming aware of the family's financial problems.

Then comes the troublesome 10th grade. Once they pass that milestone safely, a marked change takes place in the students. They become less interested in immediate requirements and more concerned with planning a personal financial future.

Students with average and below-average academic accomplishments are most likely to be afflicted with money worries. Anything that may be done to help them directly and to help them help themselves, is in the personal and public interest of all concerned.

COLLEGE COSTS

Some time ago, a close and valued friend of mine passed away. In time of trouble, for moral support, he was wont to call upon the old saying: "Things are seldom as bad as they seem." If his widow and son would have done likewise, they would have spared themselves a good deal of worthless anxiety. For there is a distinct difference between looking hopelessly at a situation, and looking hopefully into it.

My late friend had provided $5000 of life insurance for a special purpose. In the event of his death, the proceeds were to provide his son with the where-withal for a college education. When the policy was acquired, the amount seemed quite ample for the purpose it was to serve. Now the boy is ready to matriculate, but due to increased fees and the greater cost of other requirements, he fears he cannot afford to attend the one college of his choice. That troubled him and in turn his mother. Eventually, she availed herself of the advice I was able to give her, and in turn, she was able to induce the boy to alter his ideas.

Many parents are faced with a similar problem. Depending on which college is chosen, they find it will require a minimum of $500 to more than $1500 annually to cover the basic costs of a higher education. As much as 30 per cent more may have to be added to the basic figure for other essential expenses.

A breakdown of current basic college costs shows that there is ample opportunity in our country for a person to obtain a higher education at a cost commensurate with his means. In the case of the boy here in question, $1250 a year.

The survey covered all of the larger and many of the smaller 4-year institutions—550 in all—and took account of tuition and other fees, including bed and board when supplied by the school. In approximately one-eighth, basic costs were more than $1500 annually. In more than one-third, those costs were between $1000 and $1500 a year. In almost one-half, such costs ranged from $500 to $1000 a year. In about one-twelfth, the basic costs were less than $500 a year.

Literature should be obtained from a number of well-regarded and, if possible, conveniently located schools that are in a student's field of interest. Pertinent information should be segregated and carefully studied so that subsequent choices may be made if the first selection is out of the question. Any college-bound boy or girl who is able and willing to work should be able to earn several hundred dollars annually working part-time and during the summer months to supplement the means that are available.

CHAPTER V

WHERE SHOULD A WIDOW LIVE?

Soon after my newspaper column made its debut, a discussion was devoted to how and where widows live.

The reaction was immediate. Intelligent women wrote "Letters to the Editor" suggesting that some form of cooperative or club-plan housing would be an ideal way for widows to provide themselves with suitable shelter and companionship.

That, in turn, inspired more letters from widows who had large, conveniently located homes that could be converted into group housing. To quote:

"It would be a wonderful thing for lonely women. Each one could pay her way and be responsible for the upkeep of the establishment, and feel and be right at home.

"If it is possible, could you put me in touch with some of these ladies? I, too, like your column on widows. Thanks for anything you can do to help us."

"I live alone in a 10-room home, except for several roomers. I am nearly 62, but I occupy myself with many things, and I earn my own living from a small business I run in my home. Do you think it would be advisable for me to quit my business and rent all my rooms to other lonely widows who may be retired or working?"

The original suggestion about that type of tenancy was made by readers, not by this writer. A suggestion may be worthwhile or worthless. If it is practical, it should receive favorable attention. If it is inept, it should be avoided.

In my opinion, trying to operate a private residence on a cooperative or paying-guest basis for widows would not be a successful venture, unless—unless the residents consisted of women who were generally compatible in all important respects.

A group of women, more or less financially secure, who have little to do day after day except to sit around and indulge in idle and even malicious gossip and perpetual fault-finding, would not contribute to a congenial atmosphere. And that is essential. Absolutely!

On the other hand, a group consisting of business and professional women might produce a concordant circle, and would get along well enough to insure the success of such a venture. Moreover, a group of such women could be mutually helpful in a number of practical respects.

Such women are conditioned to the give-and-take of life. They would welcome a home-like atmosphere after a day's toil and turmoil. They would appreciate close companionship when they felt the need of it, and the quiet of their own rooms when they required solitude.

A few modest, well-written ads placed in the classified columns of the local press would give interested widows a pretty fair idea of what they may hope to achieve in starting and maintaining such an enterprise.

An entirely different question is raised by a lady who is thinking of selling her home and putting part of the proceeds in a house trailer. She is thinking of teaming up with her sister-in-law, also a widow, and traveling around the country until they find a place where they would like to settle. For income tax purposes, she wants to know if the purchase of a trailer would be considered as a re-investment in a home.

The answer is yes.

Depending on certain financial factors which were not revealed by her, she might or might not be required to pay income tax on these contemplated transactions. She should contact the District Office of the Internal Revenue Service for the information she should have in that respect.

INSTITUTIONS FOR INFIRM PERSONS

"I have no intention of imposing myself on my children and making them and myself miserable like so many aged and ailing widows do." That is how a woman of advanced age, recently widowed, regards her situation. As soon as her husband's estate is settled, she plans to enter a home or an institution equipped to provide her with proper care at a reasonable rate. In the meantime, she would like to have some general information on the facilities available.

For reasons of economy, convenience, congenial companionship, and peace of mind, as well as securing proper care, a number of older widows prefer to live in institutions and homes devoted to their special needs. In many cases, children who are unable or unwilling to provide care and accommodations in their own homes for their widowed mothers make the arrangements and, if necessary, assume all or part of the financial obligation involved.

There are three distinct types of homes for the aged and the mentally and physically infirm:

1. The public institutions which are maintained on the county level.

2. The philanthropic fraternal and church institutions which truly characterize provision for life care.

Admittance is effected by payment of an agreed entrance fee, and the applicant assigns property, in present or future possession, to the institution. Such institutions, in some cases, measure the efficiency of their operation with considerable care.

3. Homes for the aged and the mentally and the physically infirm. Essentially, they are commercial enterprises operated for profit. Generally, they are under the supervision of a department of public welfare.

They may not operate without a license—which is not issued unless certain conditions can be met. Each license is renewable, revokable, and non-transferable.

Usually, such an enterprise is defined as "any place of abode, building, institution, residence, or home used for the reception and the care, for a consideration, of three or more persons, who by reason of age or mental or physical infirmities are not capable of properly caring for themselves, or who are 65 years of age, or upwards."

Establishments of that type are subject to preliminary and then to regular and rigid inspections, as regards safety and sanitation. To assure adequate and proper care for each guest at all times, sufficient personnel must be provided.

Medical care of patients, nursing services, limitation as regards type of patients to be admitted to each home, food requirements, recreational facilities, guardianship of patients, admission and medical records, institutional records and reports are all considered and are definitely detailed for the guidance of all concerned.

KEEPING FARM IN FAMILY IS MANY A WIDOW'S PROBLEM

From time immemorial, keeping the farm in the family has been a matter of paramount concern to farmfolk.

Transferring a farm from one generation to the next

has become an important problem in recent years. It is a problem which concerns the 166,000 widows in the United States who own or who manage farms, as much as it does the farm family which is intact.

The technical revolution which hit farming in the recent past resulted in mechanized methods of production. Eventually, many marginal farms and farm operators were eliminated.

The successful farmers who remained, acquired much of the abandoned acreage which was adjacent to their farms to expand their operation. They purchased costly equipment to procure the most efficient production. A modern farm is in fact a modern factory representing a considerable investment in land, buildings, livestock, and equipment.

Thus, the tax problems of certain farmers—especially with respect to estate and inheritance taxes—have become more harassing. The taxes, in the event of death, are directly related to the increased value of the farm property.

In order to learn what farmers were doing to lessen the tax burden, 100 farm families told the New York Agricultural Experiment Station how they have or are planning to transfer their properties to the next generation.

The resultant report pointed out, for one thing, that life insurance could be used effectively during the transfer of farm ownership within a family to cover several specific contingencies:

1. To ease the financial strain on a farm as a going enterprise, due to the sudden passing of the owner-operator, or an operating son.

2. To avoid a forced sale of the farm in order to pay off heirs who do not participate in its operation, or to protect the interest of an operating son whose share is not large.

3. To protect the survivors of a relative-partner when a substantial part of his estate is bound up in the farm business.

About 75 per cent of the families interviewed had already transferred farms for the purposes stated, or planned to do so.

Anyone planning to do likewise would be well advised to keep the transfer businesslike, and to employ a capable, conscientious attorney to handle the legal requirements involved.

"WHERE DOTH THE WIDOW BIRD WEAVE HER NEST?"

Years ago, when I was a little lad in school, we used to recite a poem called, "Where Doth the Widow Bird Weave Her Nest?" I did not recall it until years later when, as a middle-aged man, I became concerned with thinking and writing about the problems of widowhood. Specifically, while preparing to write an article on the subject of where widows are sheltered.

But all I could recall was the question. And, as the answer might have been more fanciful than factual,

I resorted to research to reveal substantial information.

Eventually, I found the facts and an amazing analogy, but I am getting a bit beyond logical narration. First, I should mention that it was the Portuguese who settled West Africa who gave the widow birds their name. The long, black tail-feathers of the finch-weavers found there suggested the vestments of a widow (of yesteryear) to the imaginative Portuguese and, in turn, the name widow bird. The nesting or home habits of widow birds bear a remarkable resemblance to those which characterize the citizens of the civilized human community.

Some couples pair off and weave single, two-room nests in which the female sits upon her eggs in one compartment while the male occupies the other. Others build big, mushroom-shaped apartment houses to accommodate as many as several hundred tenants. Favored as house pets by some persons, a number are caught and kept confined in cages.

During the mating season, the males are decorated with tail-feathers which are five times as long as their tiny bodies. At night, when heavy dew drenches those appendages, they are unable to fly and become quite helpless. Many are then destroyed by their natural enemies. Thus, the males of the species are generally the first to pay the penalty exacted by Nature, even as are the males among mankind. And the females are left to fend for themselves and their fledglings, if any.

What of the widows of men? Where are they sheltered? They and their children? And those who are destitute, defective, and delinquent? The vast majority, more than 90 per cent, are domiciled in urban and rural non-farm communities. The rest live on farms. Those who are termed "head of household" account for approximately 60 per cent of the widows in our population. About one-third have relatives, generally dependent children living with them. One-fourth have no relatives in their homes. Most of them live alone.

Technically termed a one-person family, the widow who lives alone represents a rather difficult problem from the standpoint of analyzing a family as such. In some respects, she is just as much a family as one composed of several persons. Inasmuch as she does not have any internal relationships, her principal problem, if she is economically secure, is that of personal management.

Nearly 40 per cent of our widows live in the households of others, generally children, including sons-in-law and daughters-in-law. Considered from the standpoint of shelter, this second largest group of widows numerically is perhaps the most difficult analytically. As a subject for discussion, they provide a dilemma which may be likened to a forest of peculiar personal problems which is about as dense as it is deep.

Any one, or any number of studied situations would serve to substantiate this statement: When those who constitute this group are able to do so, they live how and where they please; otherwise, they live how and where they must, generally with a married son or daughter. As a result, many pose a trying problem to themselves and to those who give them shelter.

About 8 per cent of our widows live with other relatives, or with non-relatives as lodgers or resident employees. Two per cent are inmates of institutions: penal, mental, homes for the aged and the infirm, and philanthropic and church sanctuaries. For them, the matter of sustenance and shelter is saturated with emotional and economic implications. They reside in such institutions not from choice, but as a matter of course.

Then, there are the 2½ per cent who live here, there, and everywhere, generally in hotels, dormitories, and rooming houses.

Some three-quarters of a million widows have 1.3 million unmarried, under-18 children living with them—their own and other children who are related by blood, marriage, or adoption.

When the cherished tie that binds a husband and wife together is broken, the widowed mother must assume the duties of a father also, and account to her conscience and to society for her double-dutied administration.

Society calls them broken families, and in a way they are. But essentially, they are not broken—not as long as they have homes of some sort to give them shelter, and mothers in those homes to provide care and comfort, and income, too, in many cases.

SHOULD A WIDOW PULL UP ROOTS?

Expecting to re-establish herself quickly and easily in a new life, a new widow pulled up roots impulsively and moved elsewhere. She soon found and still feels that she erred in doing so. When she told me her story, suggesting other women might profit from her misadventure, I asked her if she would consider writing it herself. Without hesitation, she said she would, provided the names of the persons and places involved in her recitation need not be revealed publicly.

This is her story:

Losing my husband was a misfortune I could not prevent. But I blame only myself for the hardships I suffered until a few years ago. We were living in a northwestern city, and I took my husband's remains to an eastern city for burial. We had relatives there. Right after the funeral, I left the children with relatives and returned to see what I could do.

My husband was a professional man and his practice died with him. He left no business in which he had an interest that would pay me any income. Neither of us had relatives there and the friends we made no longer seemed to matter much to me.

I had three young children to look after and the insurance wouldn't last forever. I thought it all over on the train and decided to go back East to find work. I felt our relatives would help me look after the children and get settled.

The youngest child and I moved in with my sister. The older children stayed with relatives of my husband, and I started to look for work. But World War II was over and jobs were not so plentiful for a woman in my position. Before I was married, I taught school. That was long ago, and I found I would have to take a refresher course before I could teach again. That would take too long and cost too much.

To bring my children together and relieve my relatives from having to take care of them, I found rooms in the basement of an apartment building. The apartment was rent-free, and I received a small salary because I did the light janitor work.

But I found it harder and harder to make ends meet, and I had to keep using what little was left of the insurance money. To piece out my salary, I took in sewing, addressed envelopes, and baby-sat for the tenants. Living like that was not for me and my children. I decided to build a career for myself in a field in which widows were quite successful. In my spare time, I studied and prepared myself.

Then, I found an opening which I could take because my children were now older and required less attention. I worked day and night, week ends and holidays calling on prospects. I became a successful saleswoman. Financially, I now have nothing to worry about. About other problems—well, that's another story.

Looking back, I feel I could have accomplished as much if I had not pulled up roots without first considering the consequences. I could have managed as well in one place as in another until I worked things out. I wasted a lot of money traveling, moving, and getting settled in new places.

And my husband would have rested in peace wherever he was laid to rest, east or west. There is no room in a widow's life for wishful thinking. Every widow I know agrees with me. We know from experience.

SHOULD AN OLD HOME BE SOLD?

"Shall I sell it? Shall I keep it—my home?" She isn't sure. She seeks assurance. This is why: The woman who sought my advice was 67 on her last birthday. Her husband passed away a few months after they began to get their Social Security payments. Together, they received $117.80 a month. Supplemented with interest from a savings account and small sums her husband earned doing odd jobs, they managed by living frugally.

Now, she receives a widow's benefit; three-fourths of her husband's monthly payment. It amounts to $58.90. The savings were practically consumed by his last illness and the funeral expenses. The widow continues to live in the home they bought years ago. It is clear of all incumbrance. But it needs repairing, painting, and a new furnace. She has no funds for these requirements.

Living expenses take her entire income; in fact, she is constantly in debt to a small extent. That bothers her. At times, she feels she should sell the house and relieve her financial and mental strain. Located in a university district, it has a fair market value.

She has thought of remodeling it into a student's rooming house, but at her age, the whole project, in contemplation and as an accomplishment, stumps her. Besides, there seemed to be another deterrent also. Sentiment!

That she admitted after a few probing questions.

She and her husband had lived in the house for years. Their children were born there, and she wants a place for them to stay when they come to visit her, which is seldom, because they all live at a considerable distance, and none of them earns easy money.

The house as it stands, should net about $13,775. Originally, it cost $7,000. Capital improvements made over the years total some $2,000. So the cost of the property is $9,000 and the profit would be $4,775. That profit figure bears special consideration because it may be subject to income tax. In fact it is according to these figures: For purposes of the long-term capital gains tax, the profit may be reduced by 50 per cent to $2,388. That would be her adjusted gross income. Because she is over 65, she is entitled to two ($600) exemptions. Reference to the then current tax table indicated that she would have to pay a tax of $190.

With net proceeds in the neighborhood of $13,500 and somewhat more than $700 a year in Social Security benefits, she will eliminate her financial and mental strain to a considerable extent. Perhaps entirely.

What more assurance does she need?

KEEPING THE PEACE

When a widowed mother moves into the home of a married child, serious difficulties may develop. On that score alone, no widow who disrupts the home of a child can be considered a successful widow. Certainly there are exceptions, but in the course of human events, enough cases present themselves to justify discussion of the problem.

When two widowed mothers move into a home, the situation may become devastating. In fact, it did in the case of a young family when first "her" and then "his" mother did that within a year. Such a case is rather rare, but it points up the problem.

When I was told about this case, I bethought myself of a line in Hamlet: "One woe doth tread upon another's heel, so fast they follow." The person who spoke to me was a young husband who had sent a note stating he was seeking a solution for the trouble that had developed. He wanted to see me personally, and we arranged to get together one evening. He related that he was a war veteran, married seven years, and the father of two children. He had a pretty good job, was buying a small but comfortable home, and was pretty well satisfied with his lot in life until his father-in-law passed away some months ago.

Soon after, his mother-in-law came to live with them. Whether she came of her own accord or upon the invitation of his wife, he didn't know. To keep peace in the family, he simply accepted the situation. So that Grandma could have a room of her own, the two children were put together in one room. They didn't like that and became troublesome. In turn, that troubled his wife, and she became irritable.

His mother-in-law had no means to speak of. In

order to "earn her keep," she tried to make herself as useful as possible. She practically took over the running of the household. His wife seemed relieved to forego that responsibility. He resented such complete intrusion, but he continued to keep the peace.

His own parents lived in another city. When his father passed on a few months later, he brought his mother home for a visit—to help her adjust herself to her new situation. She was obliged to share the room assigned to his mother-in-law.

Soon, the mothers-in-law fell to bickering. There was a good bit of "behind-the-back" whispering in the nature of character assassination. He thought he was exercising the wisdom of Solomon when he suggested to his wife that the situation might be resolved by putting one mother-in-law and one child in each of the two bedrooms available.

But "might" did not make right. More trouble, more tension, more turmoil developed. The children retired and arose early. The grandmothers much later. They disturbed the children at night, and the children disturbed them in the morning. And that wasn't all. Unwise favoritisms on the part of the older women instilled ill-will between the children.

To add insult to the injury of his mother's pride, his mother-in-law bought some things for the house. Ostensibly this was meant to be compensation for her care, but obviously, she was making herself more comfortable. It started to look as though she intended to stay indefinitely—perhaps to spite his mother, he thought.

One day, his mother-in-law made an indiscreet remark about his mother—something about outwearing her welcome. His mother was ready with a series of sharp rejoinders. Then, the whole situation started to worsen. Eventually, his wife who was trying to walk a tightrope between and above the strife, lost her equilibrium and fell on the side of her mother. But he still kept the peace. His mother had to stick up for herself and, according to what he said, "she gave as good as she got."

Finally, his wife put it up to him, "as the man of the house," to settle the situation. He was in a quandary, in a quagmire of indecision and self-imposed impossibilities. He wanted to know what he ought to do.

I made several straight-from-the-shoulder suggestions which he was afraid to accept. So I said, "Continue to keep the peace. Leave things as they are. Eventually, the situation will settle itself." He settled for that, saying, "Somebody's sure going to get hurt in the meantime."

And my reply was: "Somebody already has; in fact, all of you have."

THE BLESSING OF CONSIDERATION

From choice or through necessity, many widowed mothers move in with married children. Some are a blessing to the homes they enter; others, a bane. The previous section told how a happy home was disrupted when two spiteful women moved in with a young couple.

"As I read about them," an acquaintance told me, "I became more grateful than ever for the happy situation in which I and my wife and child find ourselves." His words are a tribute to widowed mothers who conduct themselves with consideration when they come to live in the home of a son or a daughter.

"If my mother and mother-in-law caused us so much trouble," he continued, "I would invite them both to leave. If they wouldn't I would, and I am sure my wife would go with me.

"Our situation is quite similar to that of the troubled couple, but with one enormous difference: our mothers are angels, not monsters. I am a college student, majoring in English. My wife is working temporarily. After I graduate next year, she will go back to school to complete her studies. We were married two years ago. Just before the baby came, my widowed mother came to stay with us for a while. My wife was anxious to resume working; there was no good reason why my mother should continue to live alone in a small town, so we asked her if she would like to remain as our 'house-mother.' She was glad to.

"A few months later, my middle-aged mother-in-law, also a widow, finished her training to become a dental technician. Her husband was a dentist. After he passed on, she decided to follow in his footsteps in a manner of speaking. There were many job opportunities for her in the large city in which we lived. She came to pay us a visit and to look the situation over at the same time. In a matter of days, she was offered a splendid position, accepted it and, as a matter of course, was invited to stay with us until she could get settled in a place of her own.

"But that place turned out to be our place, by mutual consent, because we got along so well together and we all wanted to be together. I think we have a sensible financial arrangement. All of us have income from some source, even I from a part-time job and G.I. benefits. Each contributes half his earnings to a fund for house expenses. It is more than enough to cover requirements, and what each one does with what is left to him is his own business. There is no bickering about that. And I might add that when it comes to handling money, my mother is an excellent manager. So ours, at least, is one case that shows that in-laws can live together in peace, harmony, and happiness—if they are of a mind to do so. All it takes is a little intelligence and a lot of consideration for each other."

LIVING ALONE COURTS DANGER

"Why do so many widows continue to live alone in view of misfortunes that may befall them? This doesn't seem to be of enough concern to them and those who should be concerned for them. I know from reading about what happened to so many, and from what almost happened to me," says Mrs. A.T.V.

In substance this is the rest of her story and my comment:

Time was when she cherished her (so-called) independent manner of living, a burden and bother to no one, and no one beholden to her. She lived alone and liked it. Financially secure and socially satisfied, her choice was voluntary and not at all obligatory.

Then, one day, she picked up the paper and sat down to read it in the peace and quiet to which she had become accustomed. Scanning the front page, she saw a story about a widow of 71 who had been burned to death the night before in a fire that destroyed the building in which she lived. That gave her concern for her own safety. The building in which she lived was of similar structure.

Within the week, the paper published another story about a widow of 81 who tripped on a throw rug and fell down the stairway of her apartment. She was grievously injured and remained unaided until the paper boy found her hours later. More cause for concern on the part of Mrs. A.T.V., for the same thing almost happened to her.

One day, about six weeks later, she admitted a pseudo-salesman to her apartment. She was interested in what he had to offer, but was not ready to buy it. She asked him to come back in two weeks. But he seemed to be such a friendly fellow, she invited him to have a cup of tea. He accepted, and soon he was making highly improper advances toward her. All that saved the situation was the arrival of the mailman with a registered letter for which she had to sign. That was a close call and crystalized her concern for her safety.

That same day, she called the paper and inserted an ad offering to share her apartment with one or two congenial women. A number responded. She chose a widow who had a part-time job. What she pays helps with the expenses, of course, but it's of small account compared with the peace of mind which is now hers.

Reports of outrages committed upon widows are not rare. Within recent memory, two juvenile delinquents broke into the home of one, in a large city during the night, robbed her of the few dollars she had, and gave her a brutal beating.

Another, on her way home from a movie, was accosted by three hoodlums. They forced her into a truck, drove out into the country, parked on a side road, and each, in turn, assaulted her criminally.

And there have been many other misfortunes that have befallen solitary widows; even murder on occasion. Enough examples have been presented here to serve the purpose intended. If fewer widows lived alone and went about alone, fewer would be exposed to danger. For there is safety in numbers.

CHAPTER VI

BUDGETS AND BENEFITS

SPENDING ONE'S WAY TO INSECURITY

Recently I heard of a woman of wealth who went into self-pitying seclusion after her husband died. She wasted away mentally, bodily, socially. Waste of another form accompanied her decline. Hard-pressed, deserving persons were deprived of the donative good some of her money could have done.

This section deals with the plight of another woman who came into a good sum of money. She went the other way when her husband passed away. She went on a self-indulgent spending-spree that soon consumed her financial security. Her family and friends were stunned by her behavior. Those who tried to dissuade her were rebuffed—some with scorn, others with silence.

In his 54th year, while still striving abnormally to

amass more and more money, her husband died with the "bit between his teeth" as it is said. They had no children. He left almost everything to her. She was well provided for. But he neglected to protect her against a certain proclivity. She loved to spend money, go places, do things. He didn't. There had been constant contention between them about their divergent views as to what constituted the good life.

As soon as it was permissible for her to do so after her husband's demise, she started to dispose of personal property—residence, cars, furniture, and appurtenances of all sorts. What she didn't sell for a song, she gave away or threw away.

She moved into an expensive apartment, engaged a maid, bought a costly car, the finest furs, precious jewelry, and an extravagant wardrobe. She traveled whenever and to wherever she wished, took accommodations at the most exclusive hotels, played the market, played the ponies and the wheel of fortune.

But, fortune frowned more often and to a greater degree than it favored. Eventually came a day of reckoning. About 90 per cent of her assets had evaporated into thin air except for some material possessions that could be converted into cash.

She salvaged what she could, swallowed what little pride she had left, and sized up her situation. She found a job she could handle after a fashion, went to work, and moved into a modest apartment. In something less than two years, she retrogressed from a woman of means to a working woman.

For the purpose of moralizing, a suitable selection could be chosen from any number of "wise sayings," such as "A word to the wise is sufficient," or "Waste not, want not," but they seem to be old-fangled.

FEW B-R-O-K-E-N FAMILIES ARE "BROKE"

Careless tongues circulate two misconceptions regarding the financial condition of widows. One is that they are the "incarnation" of fat dividends. The other is that they are ill-off and indigent.

The first impression was given some substance by a reputable economist when he issued a statement to the effect that "all of the nation's wealth would be in feminine hands in less than 100 years." The second idea may ooze from a morass of Biblical injunctions, legal enactments and ancient adages, to the latest newspaper report of a young widow with a number of children being left destitute when her husband met accidental death.

Of course, there are widows who wade in wealth while others are poor as church mice, but extreme examples cannot be used to validate erroneous impressions.

In the main, the financial condition of a family broken by the death of its breadwinner reflects three things:

1. The earning capacity of the family (of the father only in most cases) prior to his passing.

2. His sagacity in providing income for his family in the event of his death.

3. The total thriftiness of the family group before as well as after his passing.

What does the average woman have to go on should she become a widow?

In the first four decades of this century, life insurance, as an average per family, increased from $540 to $4000—more than 600 per cent. But in 1955, the average proceeds per policy amounted to only $1349. A recent survey in one large city indicated that eight per cent of the families had less than $1000 of life insurance. Don't censure the insurance companies. Among the sellers of service, and theirs is vital, they are as aggressive as any.

A widow with small insurance proceeds should conserve the amount to the utmost and salt it away at interest to meet major emergencies. That is the wise thing to do.

Immediately, she should find out if she is eligible for Old-Age and Survivors Insurance. For herself and two under-18 children, she may be entitled to monthly payments ranging from $50.20 to $200. After the children are 18, and if she is under 62, she will receive no payments until she attains that age. Application should be made to the nearest Social Security district office.

Three other public assistance programs are in effect. While Social Security is the only one administered by the Federal government, Old-Age Assistance, Aid for Dependent Children, and Aid for the Needy Blind are operated by the states in cooperation with the Federal government.

The general rule regarding the rendering of aid under those programs is that it shall be given in relation to actual need. The nearest public welfare office will supply information. An estimated 20 per cent of the employed homemakers in the United States are widows. For that reason mention should be made regarding unemployment insurance.

It is designed to provide workers with weekly payments when they are out of work. While the system is operated by the states, the Federal government defrays the cost of administration. Complete information regarding a state's regulations and requirements may be obtained from its State Unemployment Compensation Commission. Generally, its offices are located in the state's capital city.

For the reason that a number of women are widowed as a result of fatal occupational accidents, they should be reminded that death benefits may be available to them under Workmen's Compensation. The main objective of workmen's compensation legislation is to provide payments to injured employees or to those killed in the course of employment. Specific information regarding the workmen's compensation requirements of each state may be obtained from its Industrial Commission. Its offices, usually, are located in the capital city.

Benefits are available to widows and orphans of war veterans. The Veterans Administration will assist claimants in preparing and presenting their cases in the field offices and in the central office.

It appears that the 450,000 wives who enter widowhood in an average year will have resources from various sources, in cash and in prospect, amounting to approximately 9 billion dollars, or an average of $20,-000 each. Admittedly, that is an educated estimate based on the best opinion and information available at the time it was made.

Averages may be an abomination to some people. However, the figure mentioned here indicates that as a class, widows do not roll in riches. Neither do they roll in the dust.

For many widows, life, at best, is a dismal existence. In many cases, they could shed the weary weight of lonesomeness and uselessness, but they are deterred by inertia.

On the other hand, others lose little time in taking steps to restore their shattered lives by engaging in some stimulating activity from which they derive deep personal satisfaction while providing an essential service to society.

Karen was 53 when she lost her husband. Although there was no pressing need upon her to seek gainful employment, she could not resign herself to leading a do-nothing life. Before her marriage, she had been a school teacher, and she gave serious consideration to reentering the teaching profession.

"Two factors were pretty important in my thinking," she told me. "I like to teach, and there was an urgent need of more teachers."

"Those were potent reasons," I agreed. "But were there any doubts in your mind that might have had a bearing on your decision?"

"Yes, several, but my age was the least important. Mainly, I was concerned about the present-day requirements for teaching and how I could meet them. And then, about preparing myself for teaching a subject for which I had a natural aptitude."

"I assume you reasoned that this would be to your own advantage as a student and to the advantage of your students later."

"Yes, indeed. Fortunately, I live near a large university where all the information I required was available. I checked on state and local requirements for teaching, and on the specific college programs offered for preparing teachers. I obtained copies of state certification from the state department of education. I found, as I expected, that I would have to take a refresher course. I could attend regular classes during the school year, or avail myself of the extension classes during evenings and Saturdays, and in summer sessions."

"What did you decide to do?"

"I wasn't pressed for time or money, so I decided

to attend regular classes. I wanted plenty of time to prepare and orient myself."

"What course of study did you elect to pursue?"

"I gave that a good deal of thought. At the time, in 1954, there was a substantial shortage of teachers in a number of high school subjects. English was one of the subjects, and I elected that because I had taught it previously and had a great liking for the subject."

"I presume you had no difficulty finding a position when you were ready to teach again."

"Not at all. My college, like almost every other that prepares teachers, had a placement officer who assists graduates into positions by helping school officials obtain teachers. I was offered and accepted a position in a high school in my own neighborhood, which makes it very nice for me."

In addition to teaching, Karen is continuing her own schooling to keep abreast of the constant changes in education. As a delegate, she has attended meetings of the National Education Society, and also many conferences which consider the diverse problems of aging.

In consequence of her own initiative, Karen is not living a life of loneliness and acute frustration. She is not receding into premature stages of deterioration because she, herself, saw to it that she would have the stimulation of an essential existence for herself and for society.

BUDGET FOR SELF-SUPPORTING WIDOWS

How many women work away from home? More than 21 million. How many of them are widows? Well over 3 million—many of whom are completely self-supporting and without dependents.

Even though these totally self-supporting women earn somewhat more than the average pay of all gainfully employed women, their income at best is modest. At the very least, they need enough income to cover the essential cost of living and certain comforts and conditions that totally self-supporting women may reasonably expect to enjoy.

To arrive at a cost-of-living budget, the customary requirements of such women in twelve states and the District of Columbia were considered, compiled, and averaged. The figures are fairly recent. The average annual figure for each category reflects the customary expenditure and provides a comparison pattern for all women who are similarly situated.

The average requirement per person for housing was $288.34; for food, $692.67; for clothing, $273.34; for other essentials, $437.77; for various taxes, $269.44; for savings and private insurance, $114.08. The total cost of the average, annual budget was $2,075.60.

"Other living essentials" include the items of clothing upkeep, personal care, medical, dental and optical fees, recreation including vacation, education including reading matter, transportation, and miscellaneous expenses.

In setting up the lists of goods and services that would represent the minimum requirement for an adequate, contemporary standard, the budget makers were guided by local customs. They were well aware of the pressure that is brought to bear upon the individual to conform to the customs of the group with which she is identified, as a means of securing group sanction.

Group approval is extremely important to a working woman in order that she can show herself and others that she "belongs," that she is "as good" as her associates, and that she has a "right" to be accepted on equal terms with them. In fact, her need to be identified with her group is so strong that she will, when funds are lacking, go without food, medical care, or some other essentials, in order to obtain the clothes or beauty care that will enable her to meet the standards of her group.

Inasmuch as the state budgets attempted to provide for the total financial obligations of a responsible person, they gave consideration to contingencies that cannot be included in the list of predictable requirements.

The allowance for savings and private insurance affords a means of providing, in some measure at least, for emergencies which call for unseen and unexpected expenditures.

Federal, state, Social Security, and other taxes which take an ever-increasing share of the worker's income are a part of the cost of living.

Since the payment of taxes is compulsory, if they were not provided for in the total cost of the budget, income earmarked for necessary goods and services would in reality be diverted to taxes, thus impairing the adequacy of amounts allowed for commodities and services.

MANY BENEFITS ARE NOT CLAIMED

Millions of individuals and many millions of dollars are involved in Federal Old-Age and Survivors Insurance. Every eligible survivor should claim the benefits due him when due. Still, an untold number do not, thus losing, in many cases, much needed payments in whole or in part.

Why? Because they are uninformed about survivors benefits, or their possible status as survivors, or the payments to which they may be entitled or where to apply and how to apply for the benefits.

There seems to be a reluctance to get the facts until trouble strikes. And even then, in any number of cases, the women involved do not claim the benefits which may be due them and their children because, to put it plainly, they don't know what it's all about.

In an attempt to explain, at least, the basic stipulations of survivors insurance, I have tried to simplify the involved language in which the provisions are phrased.

In the original Social Security Act of 1935, the individual rather than the family was given consideration. The 1939 amendments to the act also gave thought to his wife and dependent children. Furthermore, they made provision for benefits to his dependents upon his death. Those amendments became effective January 1, 1940.

Two classes of persons qualified for benefits were created by the 1939 amendments:

1. Those who are FULLY insured.

2. Those who are CURRENTLY insured.

The Mother's Benefit, and the Benefit for Children Under 18 in her care, grant TEMPORARY income to widows and orphans of covered workers who die fully or currently insured.

At this writing, a widow with one child may receive up to $162.80 a month; a widow with two children may receive up to $200, the top payment. The monthly payments are based on the average monthly earnings of the deceased husband.

The mother's benefit is 75 per cent of the husband's primary amount earned to the date of his death. The benefit for one dependent child is 50 per cent plus 25 per cent of the father's primary payment. The benefit for a second dependent child is 50 per cent of the father's primary payment. For example: If the father earned an average of $200 a month, his monthly (primary) benefit was $78.50. The mother's benefit is $58.90 monthly. She and one dependent child would receive $117.80. She and two dependent children would receive $157.10.

In order for the widow to be eligible for the mother's benefit, she must have been living with her husband at the time of his death. This benefit will terminate when no child is entitled to a child's benefit, or when the widow dies or remarries. Then, when she attains age 62, and if her husband expired FULLY insured, she may qualify for a widow's benefits as distinguished from a mother's benefit.

The marriage certificate, her husband's death certificate, and proof of the widow's age are required. Proof of age may be a birth or baptismal certificate, insurance policy, record of age on marriage license, or other old documents which clearly show date of birth or age.

The Social Security account number of the insured is a vitally important document. It is evidence that he had an insurance account with the United State Government. It is required in making a claim for benefits. If it is not available, his survivors who are eligible for benefits should contact his last employer, or the nearest field office of the Social Security Administration to ascertain his number. The deceased should not have had more than one such number. The Board sets up a separate account for each number issued.

Some individuals may have worked, in covered employment, since the law went into effect on January 1, 1937, without applying for an account card at any time, or until recently.

This possibility should be checked with the nearest district office of the Social Security Administration, so that credit may be received for wages earned, before the card was issued. When a beneficiary is entitled to file a claim for payments, she should go to, or write to the nearest office of the Social Security Administration stating that she wishes to claim her benefits. That office will supply the necessary application papers without charge.

SOCIAL SECURITY FOR PERSONS IN MILITARY SERVICE

Wallace graduated from a mid-western university in June, 1943. He took a long vacation that summer, and in the fall accepted a pharmaceutical position paying a good salary, plus a bonus. Although World War II was raging and he expected to be drafted any day, he and Martha, his sweetheart, were married. In no time at all, Martha was an expectant mother.

A few months later, Wallace was drafted. He had had only about five months of employment as a civilian. From April, 1944 until May, 1947, he served stateside and overseas. Unharmed in any respect by his war experience, he received an honorable discharge, returned to Martha and their boy, and took up life again as a civilian.

In the fall of 1947 he was killed accidentally. To conserve the insurance Wallace had provided, Martha went to work. She wanted to save the money for the boy's education. Hard hit by her husband's death, and worried constantly about the child's welfare while he was in the care of others, Martha was hardly fit to hold a job that paid a satisfactory salary. Eventually, she became ill and had to stop working.

She was sorely troubled until the day the personnel manager of the company she had worked for dropped in to see how she was getting along. He listened to Martha's troubles and then said, "I'd be greatly surprised if you couldn't get Social Security for yourself and the boy. Have you checked into it?" "No, I haven't," replied Martha. "Wallace worked only a few months before he had to go into the Army. Somebody told me they thought he hadn't worked long enough to get Social Security."

"At the time, that was probably true," said the personnel manager. "Your husband would have needed about one and a half years of work before Sept. 1, 1950, that could count toward Social Security. But, under the 1950 amendments to the law, Social Security wage credits of $160 a month were provided for persons in military service in World War II.

"Seems to me that you ought to be able to get something like $100 a month for yourself and the boy, based on Wallace's civilian and military wage credits."

When Martha contacted the district office of the Social Security Administration to check into her case, she was informed that she might be able to draw $105.80 a month as the benefit for a widow with one child, after making application. Martha had to supply proof of Wallace's military service and that he was discharged under circumstances other than dishonorable. That she did by presenting his discharge papers.

The Social Security Administration estimates that 240,000 mothers and eligible children of workers who died prior to Sept. 1, 1950, could now receive monthly security payments under the special provisions of the new law. Subsequent amendments continued that provision from the end of World War II through December 31, 1956.

EARNINGS WHILE RECEIVING
SOCIAL SECURITY PAYMENTS

"I am a widow getting Social Security for myself and my two children; $49.90 for me and $62.10 for the children, altogether $112 a month. Now, I am thinking of taking a job in a bakery for $160 a month to make it easier for me to manage. My sister says it is too much for me to make because it is over $1200 a year and then the Social Security would stop. Is my sister right?" asks this puzzled lady.

The sister is not right because starting January 1, 1955, a person in that position would not lose all of her Social Security benefits until she had earned more than $2080 in any one year.

Here is an easy way to figure how many Social Security payments she may get: From her total earnings in gainful employment, subtract the $1200 annual exemption and then divide the remainder by $80.

For each $80 and for each fraction of $80 in excess of the $1200 exemption, she will forfeit one payment. Examples: Earnings, $1265; exemption, $1200; excess, $65; forfeiture, 1 payment. Earnings, $1325; exemption, $1200; excess, $125; forfeiture, 2 payments. However, her children would receive their 12 monthly payments regardless.

If my figures are right, this is what she would have for the year in wages earned and in Social Security payments:

Her gross wages, $1920; her 3 unforfeited, monthly Social Security payments, $149.70, and 12 monthly payments for the children, $745.20—total, $2814.90. As a result, she would have more than twice as much income with which to manage. Moreover, from her earnings in paid employment, she may build up her own possible benefits for the time when she will be 62 and entitled to a widow's benefit.

Remember: regardless of the amount of your annual earnings, benefits are payable for any month in which you may earn under $80. In that event, you may receive payments for more than the three months cited in the example. Therefore, it may be to your further benefit to keep an accurate record of what you earn during the entire year.

At the end of the year, if your earnings have been in excess of $1200, you are required to file an annual report. The report will show your total earnings for the year, and the months in which you earned more than $80. It must be filed with the Social Security Administration not later than three months and fifteen days after the end of the calendar year. Failure to file the report within the time limit may result in the loss of additional monthly payments.

You can obtain the necessary forms from your nearest Social Security district office.

WOMEN IN DOMESTIC SERVICE

Private household work is predominantly a woman's job. The part-time workers in that occupation are mostly women who work by the hour or by the day. They number in the neighborhood of 1.7 million. About 20 per cent of them are widows forced into the labor market for economic reasons. Norma's mother is one of them.

Norma's father lost his life in the industrial plant where he had worked for a number of years. The indemnity on his life granted to his family by the State Industrial Commission was used in part to pay off the balance due on the modest home he was buying. So, his survivors are securely sheltered. They receive $136 a month from the Social Security Administration. Thus, they will not go hungry.

Norma's mother is able and willing to work outside of her home to supplement the Social Security payments. Norma is a high school student. Her brother and sister go to grade school. Her mother is busy and not too well educated, so Norma serves as the family's bookkeeper-treasurer. For a time, her mother worked for just one family, so there was no trouble about accounting for the Social Security credits due her mother. Now, because her mother works for several different families, there is some confusion in keeping the Social Security credits straight.

Norma seeks suggestions that may help her keep track of the credits to which her mother should be entitled. If her mother is paid $50 or more in cash wages by each of several employers in one calendar quarter, each employer will deduct a 2¼ per cent Social Security tax from those wages. Then, each employer will contribute an equal amount as tax for the employee's Social Security.

At the end of each quarter, each employer will report the amount of cash wages that were paid to Norma's mother, and the contribution of worker and employer to the District Director of Internal Revenue.

Obviously, Norma's mother must have a Social Security card to show to each employer. Each employer will have to see the card in order to obtain the name and Social Security number for the reports that will have to be submitted. Thus, Norma's mother will receive Social Security credits for all her earnings.

Norma should provide her mother with a small note book that can be carried in the purse. One page of the note book should be devoted to each of her mother's employers, with name, address and perhaps the telephone number at the top of the page. Then, Norma should check the note book periodically to make sure that the entries are in order. It should be kept in mind that the mother's and children's Social Security now being paid to the family is in no way related to that which Norma's mother is building up for her own account for future possible payments.

The payments now being paid to the family are based on the father's primary benefit and will be stopped altogether when the youngest child in the family becomes 18, about eight years hence, and the mother is 50. Then, no payments will be paid to the mother until she becomes eligible for her widow's benefit of $54.40 at age 62. The widow's benefit is 75 per cent of the father's primary benefit.

But, during the years which ensue, if the mother continues to work, and does not remarry, and is otherwise qualified, she may be establishing credits on her own account which may permit larger payments to her. Her benefits will not be based on her husband's primary benefit and her own earnings, but on the larger amount for the reason that she cannot receive payments from two accounts. If she should earn, for example, an average wage of $130, she may be eligible to receive payments of $64.50 monthly, or almost 20 per cent more on retirement at age 65.

AID FOR THE AGED

The purpose of this book is to help widows (and orphans), present and potential, as well as others who may have a personal or professional interest in their welfare. Therefore, the case presented here is quite in character.

The orphans in question are a man of 56 and his brother who is almost 65. Their mother is approaching 92. She has been a widow for 31 years. For many years, she was a semi-invalid. In recent years, she has been a total invalid. She requires rest home care.

In a search for the best possible care at the least possible cost, her sons have had her in three different rest homes during the last three years. They used some of her money and some of theirs to cover the cost. Now these three are almost at the end of their resources for providing the care required. Once, the cost was about $100 a month; now, it is more than $165.

At that rate, the mother's funds will last less than a year. Both sons are married. In a few months, the older will be required to retire from his job. He and his wife will have to live on a modest pension, and he will no longer be able to contribute to the care of his mother. The younger son would willingly assume the total burden of his mother's care, but it appears that he cannot do so. He and his wife work. Their combined take-home pay is about $420 a month. He is mindful of the fact that while his wife may have a moral obligation with respect to his mother, she has no legal responsibility. But she wants to help. However, their living expenses average $270 a month, including certain financial commitments which must be met.

That $270 plus the $165 required for the mother totals $435 a month—which is $15 more than their take-home pay.

The younger son wants to know if under the circumstances his mother could receive monthly assistance payments from Ohio's Aid for the Aged program. It would appear that she could. She is unable to support herself. She does not have support from a husband and imposes a considerable hardship upon her children.

She is at least 65, a citizen of the United States and has been a resident of the State (Ohio) for 5 out of the last 9 years, with the requirement of one year's residence immediately prior to application. She has no real estate worth more than $6000, and her income is not more than $960 a year. Grants may vary up to $65 a month. In addition to the monthly payments, another $200 (or possibly more starting July 1, 1956) may be granted for extraordinary medical care which cannot be met from any other source.

If a person receiving assistance dies and has no property, insurance, or any other assets, an amount up to $180 may be allowed for burial expenses. Also, any person or organization except the Division of Aid for the Aged may contribute up to an additional $70 to cover the actual cost of grave space and/or opening and closing the grave.

As soon as it is established that an individual is eligible for aid, notification is made by letter of the amount granted. Checks are mailed monthly; they

may be used according to the individual's own judgement and may not be assigned or garnisheed.

The Division of Aid for the Aged is responsible for
making readily accessible to interested persons the
opportunity of applying for assistance. It will help the
individual complete his application and secure proof
of eligibility and will, in general, assist him as needed
in exercising his rights.

UNEMPLOYMENT INSURANCE

There were almost enough widows in the United
States in 1955 to populate New York City. There were
nearly enough *working* widows to populate Chicago,
Illinois. How many of them have, at least, a working
knowledge of Unemployment Insurance? No one
knows for sure. But my own casual inquiries indicates
it rates from very vague to exactly nil.

For economic reasons, many widows must have
gainful employment. They cannot remain without
work and without funds for long without suffering
worry and in many cases a severe financial setback.
For those reasons, this section will try to offer essential information regarding Unemployment Insurance.

Suppose you are a working widow. You have lost
your job. What is the first thing you should do? Contact the nearest State Employment Service or Employment Security office in your locality to register for
another job and to file your claim for unemployment

benefits. Registering for work and filing a claim are not one and the same thing. You must do both.

If the office has any *suitable* job openings for you, you will be referred to employers who may be able to use your services. It is to your interest to investigate carefully any job possibility which the Unemployment Service selects for you.

Additionally, you are expected to attempt to obtain work on your own account. You will be told how to file your claim for unemployment benefits. Delay may result in lost benefits. Be sure to follow instructions exactly as stated. If you should move to another state or locality, you may still be entitled to benefits under certain provisions or interpretations of the law. File your claim at the nearest State Employment office in your new locality.

Benefits are paid to unemployed workers as a matter of right, not because they are able to establish need of assistance. Payments are made on a weekly basis for a specified number of weeks, and in some states, unemployment benefits continue if a worker becomes ill after filing a claim for unemployment insurance.

Unemployment Insurance laws provide for "partial-unemployment" benefits if the employer cannot provide enough work for a full week. You are covered by the law if you work in any manufacturing industry or an enterprise conducted for profit and your employer has the required number of workers, or the required number for a certain number of weeks in the calendar year. You are not covered in most states if you work on a farm, in processing agricultural products, or for a non-profit-making employer.

Generally, you have the right to receive benefits if you are laid off for lack of work, if you are able to work, if you are available for work and willing to accept any suitable job. If you have earned a certain amount of pay, or have worked for a certain time on covered jobs for the past one or two years, the amount of benefits will be related to your earnings.

In some states, you will be denied benefits if you leave your job voluntarily without good cause connected with the work, or for a reason attributable to the employer, or involuntary fault on his part. The states differ in the way they rule on claims of women who can work on certain shifts and not on others, or who otherwise must limit the conditions under which they will accept work.

STATE WORKMEN'S COMPENSATION LAWS

Under State Workmen's Compensation Laws, only two states recognize the financial plight in which a family may find itself when the father is killed, and provide for an immediate lump sum payment.

To the widow, Mississippi authorizes the immediate payment of $100 in addition to other compensation benefits. Under a similar type of provision, North Dakota grants $300 to the widow and $100 to each dependent child up to a maximum of $600.

The purpose of death benefits is to provide for those who have been dependent upon the deceased workman. The amount of compensation awarded and the maximum period of payment vary to a considerable extent under the different laws.

However, in the District of Columbia, Hawaii, several states, and under the Federal employee's and the longshoremen's act, the laws provide for the payment of benefits to a widow for life, or until remarriage, and in the case of dependent children until a specified age has been reached.

The other states limit the payment of death benefits to a specified period ranging from 260 to three times that number of weeks. But in some cases, payments continue to children until they reach a specified age, generally 18.

In one of those states, payments continue to the widow during periods in which she is not, in fact, self-supporting. Some of them also limit the total maximum payment which may range from $4,000 to $20,000 for a widow and children.

Generally, the compensation laws base the death benefits on the average weekly wages of the deceased worker. In a few states, a flat amount is paid, while in one state and one territory, a lump sum is paid.

All of the compensation acts provide for the payment of burial expenses subject to a specified maximum amount ranging from $150 to $500. In four states and Puerto Rico, the payment of such expenses is limited to cases where there are no dependents. In one, the maximum varies according to whether or not there are dependents.

The principal purpose of workmen's compensation is to eliminate the uncertainties of collecting indemnities at common law or under the employers' liability laws. Before the workmen's compensation laws were adopted, dependents got little or nothing in recompense. To recover damages from employers, they had to file suit and prove that their loss was due to the employer's negligence.

The employer, even though negligent, could avail himself of three common law defenses: if it was proved that the employee's death was due to the ordinary risk of his work, if it was caused by the negligence of a fellow worker, or if the employee by his own negligence contributed in any way to his death.

The compensation laws reduced the rigorous defenses which the employer could use. But in spite of the employers' broadened responsibility, results to the claimants were still unsatisfactory. They still had to bring suit against the employer and prove that the fatality was his fault. There were still long delays in securing court action, uncertainty of results, and the high cost of negligence suits. Often, the dependents were denied any compensation or damages. With the passage of compensation laws, claimants were assured payments of benefits regardless of fault, and with a minimum of legal formality.

Life is beset with big and little fears from which few persons are exempt. Women certainly have their share, and widows, as a class, have some that are singular in nature.

Perhaps the best way for an individual to cope with a problem is to try to think it out alone. When the pros and cons seem to exert equal power, it helps to have the opinion of an interested person who is not directly involved in the matter. In certain cases, that will counteract the personal prejudices that may sway one from a course that may lead to a successful solution. That is why two women turned to me. One is a widow. The other fears she will be soon.

The widow's husband was a fairly wealthy man. During his life, he was a philanthropic person, and certain charities were well remembered in his will. His estate was unusually involved, and by the time it was settled, there was less available to her than was anticipated. However, there is a general assumption that she is better off financially than she actually is.

She is constantly solicited for more and more money by more and more fund raisers, and has finally reached a point where some must be refused unless she withdraws assistance she is rendering to less fortunate members of her own family. She fears that this will cast unfavorable reflection upon her from two directions. A sensitive, conscientious person, she was not above asking for advice that might ease her mind.

First, I reminded her that "charity begins at home." Then I suggested that she take careful account of her anticipated annual income and set aside a proper percentage for all charitable purposes, public and private, and stop with that. Finally I said, "A successful businessman such as your husband was probably found it necessary to say 'no' as often as he said 'yes.' After due consideration, of course. It appears you will have to learn to do likewise."

The other woman has a problem that is diametrically opposite the case first cited. Her husband is alive and able to earn a fair living. But he has an incurable disease and is not insurable. He may live for years and he may not. Her own health is not too good, and she fears for her future. Her attitude is suicidal. To offer possible help, I told her of two similar cases that came to my attention some years ago.

The husband of one woman was a small businessman, that of the other was a mechanic. The men were friends of mine, and felt able to discuss their cases quite candidly.

To each one I suggested that under the circumstances he had no choice but to try to insure himself. I remember telling them to put every penny they could spare in some safe form of savings, such as United States Savings Bonds.

Both men passed away recently. By the time they expired, their savings and interest, plus Social Security benefits, provided their widows with about as much protection as the average man with a fair income is able to carry.

CHAPTER VII

EMPLOYMENT OPPORTUNITIES

EMPLOYMENT OPPORTUNITY INDEX

Some widows have no choice but to work. In many families, they constitute the final defense against economic defeat. Others work to supplement insufficient income received from other sources. Still others, in more fortunate circumstances, want to work to consume excess physical energy and to maintain mental health. For the vast majority of widows who must or who want to work, consideration of actual abilities and liabilities is certainly of prime importance. Then, consideration should be given to the more ordinary occupations and opportunities that exist.

For that purpose, data assembled by the Bureau of the Census, which were analyzed by the Women's Bureau of the Department of Labor, offer good guidance. The count considered approximately four million gainfully employed homemakers, and the information was compiled according to seven major classifications and one miscellaneous group. On the basis of that information, I constructed an employment opportunity index for widows to indicate the relative ease with which each field may be entered.

First, the number in each classification was considered as a percentage of the four-million total. Then, the percentage of widows in each classification was computed. The two percentages were combined to produce the index figure. On that basis, the index organized itself in the following order:

1. *DOMESTIC SERVICE*. There is always a market for such help. Experienced, older women predominated.

2. *INDUSTRY*. The natural dexterity of women is essential to employment in many lines of manufacture. Here, too, women of older age were dominant.

3. *AGRICULTURE*. Farm wives participate in producing family income to a greater extent than any other class of women. When they become widows, they generally continue in their normal occupation as a matter of course, if they do not dispose of their farms.

4. *OFFICE WORK*. The business office is the more or less recognized realm of the working girl. Almost every kind of job requires special skill which must be acquired through experience or training. Most older

women have neither the time nor the temperament to prepare for office work. Even women of relatively young old age are reluctant to enter this field in which the ability to "wear" clothes and apply cosmetics cleverly provides too much "competition."

5. *PROFESSIONAL WORKERS.* Ability and not age is all that counts in this field. In fact, it seems to be a case of the older the better. That is not surprising in view of the fact that professional skills generally improve with age.

6. *SELLING.* The percentage of employed homemakers in this field is comparatively small. High-caliber, high-pressure salesmanship is almost altogether a man's field, and a woman cannot very well instigate or participate in the "entertainment" and fraternization that generally ensues when men get together on big deals.

Generally, the retail field offers the woman who is interested in selling the most satisfactory opportunities. Here, she is on familiar ground, and the larger retail establishments offer not only valuable training, but almost constant inducement to increase earnings.

7. *EMPLOYED AT HOME.* This category is comprised of women who prefer to work on their own premises, operating all manner of small commercial and professional ventures.

8. *MISCELLANEOUS.* This is a rather difficult group to analyze. Conjecture would say that this "all sorts" group consists mainly of the two extremes of employed homemakers: those with such limited abil-

ity that they accept the least attractive employment, and those who are particularly qualified to engage in some extraordinary occupation.

Usually, it is the older widow with substantially higher earnings who is the sole support of her family. Odd, isn't it, that the dubious advantages of advancing age and widowhood should work to the benefit of women who are the sole support of their families?

GETTING A JOB IS A JOB IN ITSELF

Medical progress and improved standards of living have increased the life span of both men and women. But women on the average live longer than men, and more and more women work and continue to work until retirement, even as men do. The percentage of women who are gainfully employed has been increasing steadily over the last ten to fifteen years. While some work as a matter of choice, many must when they are suddenly and involuntarily forced to support their families and themselves.

In 1955, 40 per cent of 7.6 million widows worked at full-time and part-time jobs. More than 25 per cent of the 2.7 million women in the 65-69 age group were working. More than 10 per cent of the 4.7 million in the over-70 age group were working. So, the matter of job-finding for the mature woman, and especially the widow, merits consideration. For it has been said and it is often true that getting a job is a job in itself. If a woman is prepared to work and is looking for a job, it would be greatly to her advantage to avoid hoping and groping, and to proceed according to a plan.

Her plan should be a two-part program: 1) Finding some good job opportunities and 2) arranging interviews with prospective employers.

Part one should include these ideas:

1. Question relatives and friends for leads to good job openings.

2. Obtain advice from competent counselors and experienced placement interviewers who know the local labor market and who will take an interest in placing you.

3. Check with the State Employment Service, college placement bureaus, women's business and profession groups and other non-profit agencies.

4. Watch the newspapers for leads such as new industries, stores, and institutions coming into the community, and expansion of established enterprises.

5. Check the "help wanted" ads in the newspapers, trade journals, professional magazines, and the self-employment opportunities advertised in the women's service magazines.

6. Apply in person, or by phone or letter to former and prospective employers. Request a personal interview.

Part two should include these ideas:

1. Personal data sheets to leave with prospective employers. Give your name, address, phone number, and concise summary of education and experience in paid and unpaid employment.

2. Knowledge of prospective employers; specifically, stability and standing, products and services, names of officials—especially personnel and employment managers.

3. Papers to take to interviews should include personal data sheet, Social Security card, references, samples of work or other evidence of ability, diplomas, certificates, and membership cards that may have a bearing on employment.

4. Be prompt for interview, and confident but modest. When interview is over, leave with a polite "thank you," and do not apologize for your age.

More and more employers are becoming aware that suitably placed, mature workers are more loyal, stable and responsible. And more efficient. They have found that the loss of productive capacity that may come with age in some cases is slight and is usually compensated for by other assets and virtues.

PART-TIME WORK

A few facts can certainly sink a shipload of speculation. Regarding part-time jobs for women, I would have said, offhand, that widows would be in the majority. But when I saw and studied a Census Bureau report of the work experience of the population in 1955, I learned that they were in the minority.

It is married women who are predominant in part-time occupations. They account for more than two-thirds of such workers, single women for one-fifth, and widows for one-tenth. Numerically, widows are of least importance, but that cannot be taken to mean insignificant, especially in our field of interest.

From the figures, I would say that some 750,000 widows are engaged in gainful, part-time employment. A special survey made in ten selected cities supplies some pertinent information on this particular subject.

Although added income was an important factor in some cases, many widows placed more than monetary value on a part-time job for this significant reason: It helped them to overcome loneliness.

Those who most keenly felt the need for interests and contacts outside their homes were mature women without dependent children, or whose children were grown, or nearly so; women who were financially secure, or substantially so. Friends, relatives, and former employers were instrumental in helping most of those women find part-time jobs.

In clerical, sales and service work, approximately 40 per cent got job leads from friends and relatives; 50 per cent approached former employers directly, the rest answered "help wanted" ads in newspapers and contacted possible employers. Nurses found that former employers and direct application were equal to the leads from friends and relatives in their search for part-time employment. As for social workers, 70 per cent gave credit to former employers and social agency contacts for their job leads and eventual employment. Teachers found that direct applications were as useful as friends in obtaining employment. University placement agencies and former employers were of secondary importance.

Fewer than 10 per cent of the women seeking placement in part-time jobs were directed by private and public employment agencies, including school placement bureaus. Some of the women, principally teachers, stenographers, and bookkeepers stated that they did not find their part-time jobs, but that their jobs found them. A part-time job is a morale builder for any widow with the time, energy and the urge to "do something" for her community through welfare agencies and civic and church organizations. Even though their earnings in many cases did not cover the expenses incurred, they derived greater satisfaction in being recognized as regular, responsible, paid staff members.

More important than personal satisfaction, however, is the economic fact that there are many capable, well-trained women willing to work part-time in fields that are sorely handicapped by a scarcity of trained personnel. Opportunity to use her skill combined with her sense of social obligation will give many a widow a wholesome outlet for any feelings of lonesomeness and uselessness she may harbor.

EMPLOYMENT FOR OLDER WOMEN

Now comes Mildred who states that she must find a job for two reasons. The first is that she can use the money. The second is that she can't go on wasting her life and feeling sorry for herself. Her husband died two years ago. Her two daughters are married and live in distant cities. One son is in the Navy, the other travels with a name band. She sees none of her children very often, has few intimate friends and relatives to whom she feels close.

"I am sure that pleasant work that pays fairly well will solve a good deal of my problem," says Mildred. "But I am now 58, and never worked for money after I was married 36 years ago. Before that, I only had one job, an easy one as secretary to a business executive. I am wondering if I should try to get a job as a secretary again. My typing is still pretty good, because I used to do quite a bit of it for my husband. But, to tell the truth, my shorthand is pretty bad. Also, I am wondering now how I would fit into a business office at my age."

First, Mildred is to be commended for her sensible outlook on her situation, and for making a definite decision to do something about it. Second, as to secretarial work, it was noted in a previous discussion that the business office was the domain of the working girl. So much so, that even young "older" women hesitate to try that field. However, circumstances alter cases. Currently, office help of all kinds is in short supply.

Employers who were more interested in a pretty face and figure than in a worker's ability are undergoing a change of mind, if not a change of heart. A considerable number know that ability to do a job, stay with a job, and stay on the job is really all that counts. So, that 35 age limit notion is wavering. And being waived. If Mildred's heart is set, as it seems to be, on being a secretary again, she should by all means venture it. But she will have to invest some time and perhaps money in preparing herself. The admonition should be taken seriously, because she may possibly find it easier to get a job than to hold it. Business is business.

In a number of the larger cities, in addition to the commercial schools, vocational training classes are being offered in trade and high schools. Women of legal age are eligible for daytime and evening classes. In many cases, the training is free. In some states, there is small fee for materials and textbooks, and women over 21 may be charged a small fee. Generally, the schools admit applicants referred by the State Employment Service. Except in the case of women who are not sure of their skills, entrance tests are not a requirement. The simple statement of a candidate to the effect that she has knowledge of typing and shorthand is sufficient, usually, to gain her admittance.

Courses are planned to cover a certain period of time in weeks or months, and classes convene according to a definite schedule. Trainees are not required to attend the entire scheduled term of a refresher course.

Training in office techniques, as well as the special refresher course in shorthand and typing, are provided. If Mildred is interested in the vocational training program, she should write to the State Director of Vocational Training. Those offices are usually located in the capital city. It would be well for Mildred to keep in mind that business offices are not the only ones that have need of proficient secretaries. There are also the professional, educational, and religious offices to be considered. An older woman might be quite content to work in such an environment. In fact, it would be highly advisable for any older woman who wants to enter or re-enter secretarial service to prepare herself for a definite sort of a job in congenial surroundings.

PRACTICAL NURSING

Among all manner of nursing personnel, the prospect for the practical nurse has changed most favorably. Extraordinary developments in the scope of training opportunities are evident. New requirements for licensing and standards of practice are in effect. The entire effort has definitely raised the level of practical nursing. Candidates who are now or who have been married are considered prime material for training as practical nurses. They are preferred because of the information and experience they may have acquired in household management and home nursing care.

That may be significant news for many of the 2.2 million widows who are in the 45 to 65 age group. Public school systems providing practical nursing programs as a part of adult education, admit older women up to 50 years of age, if they can qualify with respect to aptitude and physical requirements. The matter of upper age limit is left open in many schools if the admission committee finds the applicants suitable in other respects.

Broadly, there are three types of approved schools offering training for practical nurses: Those operated by the public-school system as part of a state or local vocational or adult training program; privately operated schools affiliated with hospitals and health agencies, and schools operated by hospitals exclusively.

In the public school system, the cost of training ranges from no fees to $100 or more. If a student needs to earn her keep, public school authorities will approve part-time employment if it will not impair the trainee's health or interfere with her training.

In the case of hospital training, it is sometimes possible for the student to obtain a maintenance allowance. Some hospitals provide room, board, and laundry in lieu of an allowance.

Most private, non-profit vocational schools for practical nurses make a charge for tuition. Fees vary considerably from place to place. Therefore, women who are interested in a particular private school should inquire regarding the charges. At least nine months of preparation in an approved school is required to become a practical nurse. In some states, the requirement is as much as 18 months. Generally, the training period is 12 months, or 2000 hours. Periodic surveys made by the American Hospital Association indicate the average starting salary for practical nurses was $164 a month. That would be about 70 per cent of the average starting salary for professional nurses on general duty.

Reliable information concerning the earnings of practical nurses employed in private homes or physicians' offices is not available. However, the director of an approved school in Washington, D. C., reported that graduates of that school expected to earn from $7 to $8 daily, with one meal and carfare for duty in private homes, and $1 for each hour under eight. The daily rate for 12 hours of duty tended to be approximately $10.

The stringent need for practical nurses offers women of mature age an opportunity for occupation that is certainly good from the standpoint of attaining a gratifying status at a time of life when most older women are content to just coast along.

The easiest way to obtain information about practical nursing schools is from the State Board of Nursing Education. Another source is the National Association for Practical Nurse Education, 654 Madison Avenue, New York 21, N. Y.

HIGH LEVEL POSITIONS HELD BY WIDOWS

In all fields of employment, many higher-level positions which were once considered "men's jobs" are now held by women, a number of whom are widows. According to a sample survey of the nation-wide situation: In department stores, 7 per cent of the more responsible positions available to women were filled by widows. In the main offices of insurance companies, 5 per cent of the executive, semi-executive, and specialized jobs open to women were held by widows. In the banking business, 3 per cent of thirty-one kinds of higher-level opportunities open to women were occupied by widows. In manufacturing firms, 6 per cent of a long list of responsible duties suitable for women were being discharged by widows. Considering that widows constitute 12.2 per cent of our country's female population, 14 and over, that is a comparatively significant showing.

For women who want to improve their financial security and personal satisfaction by means of a more responsible career in the commercial world, that is inspiring information.

The remainder of this section will consider, briefly, the various avenues along which women have achieved their present responsible positions. Since individual achievement is the result of so many factors not easily defined, any attempt at generalization is admittedly difficult. Only one thing was common to most of them —a love of their jobs.

When asked what they liked about their jobs, some of the women answered "everything," and conversely, when asked what they disliked, many more answered "nothing." Repeatedly, the women interviewed spoke of the satisfaction of holding a challenging and responsible position which gave them recognition with regard to their capabilities.

Particular job requirements as well as possibilities for advancement varied extensively with the kind of work being performed. As might be expected, the women in all fields who had reached the higher-level jobs were an older group than women workers in general. Three-fourths of the women were 35 years or older, in contrast to about half the women in the labor force. Women in the more responsible positions covered by the survey were not predominantly college-educated. In department stores, nearly half of the women, and in other industries considerably more than half, had not more than a high school education.

It would appear, then, from the foregoing findings, that experience and specialized on-the-job training plays an important part in fulfilling the requirements for higher-level positions, especially so when a limited general education must be supplemented. The women holding higher-level positions were to a considerable extent persons with extensive work experience. In all fields, about two-thirds of them had been working for more than fifteen years. It is apparent that women who hold the more responsible positions take a marked interest in their work and make extraordinary efforts to be successful at it. The vast majority of the women questioned believed they owed advancement to their present positions to having discharged their duties successfully. When asked what other women should do to get ahead, almost without exception they advised "better work performance and attitudes," as well as "ambition or desire to succeed."

The retail business has an ancient axiom which affirms that "merchandise which is well bought is half sold." It has another of more recent coinage which asserts that "merchandise that is well displayed is half sold." Taken together and integrated with intelligence and industry, those basic ideas would almost assure the success of any business enterprise.

Those are the principles by which a small but popular children's shoe store in San Mateo, California, is operated.

The store is run by Mrs. Harriet Carley. She and her husband operated a family shoe store in Sheridan, Wyoming, until his passing some years ago. Before moving to San Mateo, she managed the children's footwear department of a store in San Francisco. So, when it comes to selling shoes, Mrs. Carley is not a neophyte.

It would seem that the manner of her merchandising would set a good example for other women who are engaged in operating small businesses which cater to somewhat specialized classes of customers. Her ingenuity inspires ideas for store decoration and stock displays that are remarkably attractive and appealing. Her do-it-yourself abilities enable her to take the most prosaic things, some salvaged from junk, and convert them into clever devices for displaying merchandise.

Many of the things Mrs. Carley uses cost next to nothing, but they are definitely effective in promoting sales. Moreover, in contriving them, she keeps herself constructively occupied, which is essential for women in her position.

One unusual display was built upon and around an antiquated foot-powered sewing machine and a child's rocker that were sprayed with a pleasing shade of paint and finished off with touches of gilt.

For fitting the small fry with shoes, safely and at a comfortable height, Mrs. Carley built a tier of four waist-high seats decorated with animal pictures and equipped with "safety" belts. The youngsters occupy the seats only long enough to be fitted; then they are placed on the floor. A child is never left alone upon a seat. Either the mother or a clerk remains watchful.

To keep her pre-school customers occupied, Mrs. Carley has a supply of nursery books on a small school-desk-and-chair set. Once scheduled for the discard, it was refinished and now serves to help sell shoes. She also finds that giving a child a lollipop is a good way to make him more co-operative.

The entrance to her store is adjacent to a small court near the front of the building. That leaves almost the entire expanse of frontage available for window display purposes.

As might be expected, the exceptional talents of Mrs. Carley are vitally evident in her window displays. A unique display piece, fashioned of white-finished wrought iron and topped with glass, was once an obsolete coffee table. While not obtrusive, it is the highlight of a window that is arrayed with many interesting materials native to the area to add spice to the displays of shoes and related merchandise. For accent effect, small shadow boxes, the product of this versatile woman's own handiwork, are set into one of the interior walls. These are used to give "picture" emphasis to seasonable styles. A huge mirror opposite the entrance and light-tinted walls and ceiling give the effect of enhancing the size of the store. To show shoes in season, and to protect the displayed shoes from becoming sun-scorched, the window is changed completely each week.

One of Mrs. Carley's pet projects is reclaiming discarded shoes for needy children—serviceable shoes which have been quickly outgrown by other children. While she does not salvage such shoes for the sake of publicity, it would be difficult to evade the favorable comment evoked by her consideration for children who cannot always have new shoes.

In Mrs. Carley, we see a woman who is ambitious, energetic, conscientious, self-reliant—in short, a success.

ADVERTISING, GOOD DISPLAY ESSENTIAL

One Saturday forenoon some months ago, my wife took her life in her hands and interrupted me when I was deeply engrossed in my writing. It seems she had forgotten to buy and mail a birthday present for one of our grandchildren who lives in another city.

"Do you suppose you can stop a little while and run me out to that children's specialty shop in the new shopping center?" she asked. "That nice little store that was started by that woman whose husband passed away about a year ago."

Taking everything into account, I couldn't very well refuse. Arriving at the store, I said to my wife, "You go on in. I'll wait in the car. I want to think about something."

She wouldn't buy that, so I trailed along. In the store, while I was waiting, I struck up a conversation with the proprietress, the widow my wife had mentioned. I knew her slightly. My opening gambit was the usual trite question: "How's business?"

"Well," she replied, "I can't complain about anything except the shoes. I am afraid I made a bad mistake when I put them in."

"Shoes!" I said with some surprise. "Why, I didn't know you carried shoes. I've passed by here any number of times, and I've never seen as much as a shoe-lace in your window."

I looked around and saw some shoe boxes on several shelves at the back of the store. They were almost obscured by other merchandise and display devices. "You certainly ought to sell children's and baby shoes here," I observed. "Why there are more kids and expectant mothers around here than——"

"That's what I thought, too," she broke in, "but they just aren't moving as they should."

"Maybe it's because you aren't trying to move them as you should," I answered. "You've got coats, dresses, undies, and what-not in your window display. Why no shoes? You've got to show to sell. And come to think of it, I've never seen an ad of yours in the neighborhood paper."

She started to say something, and I guess I took the words out of her mouth.

"Sure, it's fine and dandy for you to know that you have a nice line of children's shoes in your store. But are you sure the people around here really know that? How can they if you don't show them and tell them? Why, it's almost impossible for anyone who's right in the store to see you carry shoes!"

"I don't think I can afford to advertise," she replied. "Advertising costs money."

"So does rent, light, water, heat, and everything else. The way I see it, you can't afford not to advertise. For one thing, you can put some shoes in your window along with the other things. That won't cost you anything.

"For another, you can move your shoe stock up front, here, where people can see it, and put some of that staple stuff back there where the shoes are. That won't cost you anything."

On the way home, my wife said, "You were having quite a chat with that woman. If it wasn't too confidential would you mind letting me in on the secret?"

So I told her what the little confab was about and added: "That's the trouble with so many of those small merchants. They just don't seem to understand what is involved in modern merchandising. Especially in so many small-town and neighborhood stores that wouldn't get to first base if it weren't for the fact that they are convenient. With so many of them, doing a good sensible job of advertising involves two bad words: spending money."

When we were back home, I referred to a report that stated that nearly a million women were engaged in business as proprietors, officials, and managers. Another report showed me that about 10 per cent might be widows.

"Two years after we were married, my husband and I bought a small business. He operated the plant and I took care of the office. We were short of operating capital and had no money to make capital improvements, so we took in, as a silent partner, a friend who had money. That eliminated the struggle we were having, and we started to make headway. Then, four years later, my husband took sick suddenly and died," states Mrs. Ellen M.

The rest of her letter is herewith summarized. Not

before her husband's death and not since has the silent partner been in a position to take an active part in managing the business. The widow had to assume the total responsibility. In the twenty-odd years that have passed, the business has expanded to the point where it is worth approximately 150 times the original investment, thanks to her enterprise. She has accomplished what she set out to do, is tired, but not ready to retire yet. When she retires, or if she expires before that time, she wants to leave the business in competent hands.

Her daughters are married to successful professional men who would hardly be interested in coming into the business.

Her son has worked for her for a number of years. He has a good job and is doing a good job in the plant. "He knows the business as well as I do," she says, "but he is not a salesman or a businessman. I am thinking seriously of bringing him into the office and training him to take over, but I'm scared stiff to try it, or even to talk to him about it. He might not make good, and he might not be interested in the project in the first place.

"You're a businessman, Mr. Zalk. What would you suggest?"

Obviously, Mrs. M., you have belatedly become aware of the fact that when a business interest is to be retained after death, or after retirement, the succeeding management is a matter of prime importance. Let's start probing into a possible solution to your problem with an old business proverb: "Nothing ventured, nothing gained."

You ventured and you gained when you and your husband started your business; why not venture with your son—granted that it is often easier to talk with and deal with strangers?

He is active in the business, he knows the business. No doubt he eventually will inherit a share of it, so why not arrange to give him a share now to increase his interest and to develop whatever latent business abilities he has?

To bolster your position and your son's, it would be advisable to give certain key individuals an opportunity to acquire an interest in the business now, or at the time of your retirement, or in the event of your death.

There is no substitute for experience, and loyal workers are worth all you can afford to do for them. It is altogether in your interest to give such persons added incentive and opportunity to profit from their industry and ability.

With regard to your silent partner who has no doubt profited handsomely over the years from his small initial investment, it would be well to have a basic understanding with him concerning what you have in mind. And it should be understood by the other members of your family that the survivor who manages the business is entitled to receive adequate compensation for his services before any earnings are shared.

CHAPTER VIII

LONELINESS...THE PRIME PROBLEM
OF WIDOWHOOD

WEALTH NO ANTIDOTE FOR LONELINESS

Lack of sufficient funds seems to be a perpetual problem with many widows. Yet, a widow may have as much as a million dollars at her disposal to do with as she pleases, and still be disconsolate. For instance, this unfortunate soul:

She was an aged person living, not in state, but in a solitary state, in her mansion. She was clad in rags and so weak from hunger that she crawled around the place like some trapped wild creature. The details of this case were disclosed in a court of jurisdiction.

Widow of a former official of a famous manufacturing firm, she had traveled abroad numerous times in her younger days, After her husband's death, she returned to her magnificent home and lived in seclusion for fifteen years.

A near relative intervening in the case told the court of a visit to the woman's home, where he found $200,000 in uncashed dividend checks which had accumulated over the years. He filed a petition asking that the woman be made a ward of the court, and that an administrator be appointed because she was not capable of managing her own affairs.

The court was informed that the woman's own estate was worth at least $700,000 and that in addition she was receiving a life income from another $500,000 estate. Another amount, approximately $65,000 was found in a savings account.

A former chauffeur for the widow testified she had become so dejected after her husband's death that she would not leave the house. "She talked of two phantoms always being in the house and attempting to poison her," he affirmed.

Here was a woman whose financial security was assured. It is reasonable to assume that during her husband's life he lavished every luxury and attention on her that money and prestige could command. She was his life, and when he left this life, she was a lost child. A poor little rich girl.

Great wealth is a great responsibility. She should have been conditioned and counselled to use some of hers to help others who were far less fortunate in the matter of money.

For instance, she could have helped the ill and the

indigent among the 28,000 widows and the 60,000 orphans in her own city during the years she was possessed by self-pity to such a degree that she departed from normality.

ANTIDOTE FOR LONELINESS

"If the choice could have been given her,
She would have said without debate,
He might be lonely should I go away,
Let me be the one to wait."

Some years ago, when I first started to contemplate the problems of widowhood, I came across that touching little poem on the editorial page of the *Columbus Dispatch*. Written by Pauline Saeger, it expresses a degree of composure that any widow would do well to practice. If we read the poem rightly, we picture a wife who gracefully has become resigned to the loss of her life's companion. And she wanted to spare him loneliness—the primal and prolonged problem of those who are widowed.

Considering the character of the person, as revealed by the sentiment, we may conjecture that she would be admirably able to sublimate the loneliness of her lot. How? By disliking self-imposed pity and devoting herself to a life of serving those who are sorely in need —those with whom she could feel a sistership in sorrow. Thus, she would not remain unwelcome, uninvited, unwanted, and lonely.

Such a woman would be the Detroit widow who

raised her own child, ten adopted children, and foster-mothered thirty-four others. She is Mrs. Jane Maxwell Pritchard, age 67, social worker, civic leader, and spiritual guide who was named American Mother of 1956. Of the forty-five children, only one, son Dale, age 38, is hers by birth. Ten came to her by formal adoption. The others, all girls, have lived with her for different periods of time in her role as foster parent for the Juvenile Court of Detroit. They all came from broken homes.

Mrs. Pritchard's family is a rather remarkable group. The "oldest" child, an adopted daughter, is 43 while the youngest of the adopted children are 14-year-old twins. One of her three adopted sons died while he was yet a youth. Her husband, Benjamin, passed away in 1947. Some of the young girls entrusted to Mrs. Pritchard by the Court have continued to live with her for years. Others remained until they were married, and the weddings were held at her home. Out of regard for her, some of the girls have even taken her name.

From her own son, who should know Mrs. Pritchard best of all, came this tribute: "It was a privilege to be one of her children, to share in her love and attention. She is something to marvel at, and my most prized possession."

Self-inflicted loneliness is a form of self-poisoning which may damage one mentally and physically. There is an effective antidote for those who are over-anxious about their state of solitude. This is it: Look forward to the new days that are yet to come, and not back upon those that have vanished forever. Look upward to the star of hope, and not downward in despair and dejection. Look about and seek out those who are friendless, kithless, homeless. Be of good heart, and to them be a good friend.

WIDOWS ANONYMOUS

Clare is a person who feels that a new widow's family and friends ought not to concern themselves too much about her state of mind. "In trying to help her forget her misfortune," she says, "they may do more harm than good. In my case, for instance, the attempts made to distract me were so obvious that they had an opposite effect, and in one instance the result was so horrible that some of those involved suffered a good deal of humiliation."

Clare is a young woman who works as a librarian. She lives with a married sister. "One day while helping a student gather reference material for an essay on bird life," she continued, "I came across something so descriptive of my own and similar situations that I could hardly believe my eyes. I learned that magpies have a strange way of supplying new mates to bereaved birds within a day or two. It seems that as soon as the sad news is broadcast, a great number of the species gathers on the scene, and apparently the new mate is selected from among those present."

I anticipated the amazing analogy before Clare put

it into words, but I did not interrupt her, and she seemed to be somewhat vengeful when she said: "There I had a perfect picture of my family and friends—just like a flock of meddling, chattering magpies.

"Right after Stan's funeral, I became project No. 1. Everyone was extra-nice, extra-attentive, and over-concerned. In order to avoid offending and to appear grateful, I accepted their attentions and invitations reluctantly.

"There was plenty of propaganda. I was reminded that I was young, told I was nice looking, advised to lead a normal life, and assured that in due course I would meet someone. The implication was plain enough."

"I presume there was some effort made to bring that about," I said.

"Oh, yes, my brother-in-law is quite a promoter. He and my sister and a group of our friends celebrated last New Year's with a dinner party at a large hotel. I was invited to attend, but excused myself. However, I was literally talked down and dragged out of the house. We started for the hotel rather late and by the time we arrived, our friends were 'full of good spirits,' as my brother-in-law put it. Then, he introduced me to a fellow who was loaded with liquor and ideas about me. He wrapped his arms around me, kissed me, said he had been dying to meet me and in a loud voice told me I would never be a poor, lonesome little widow as long as I had him for a friend. To avoid creating a scene, I controlled myself. It wasn't easy. As soon as the oaf released me, I left the hotel and went home."

"Perhaps the others in the party were too amazed or too amused to interfere," I suggested.

"That's what they told me later," she said.

Clare feels that widows, particularly new widows, should have attention, but it should be of a kind that is not harmful but helpful like Alcoholics Anonymous or Divorcees Anonymous, which are groups of people who can be helpful because they have learned how to cope with certain problems.

I was surprised and pleased to hear her tell me that she visits newly bereaved women on occasion and that her helpful concern is good for them and for her.

"It would be a fine thing if every community had a Widows Anonymous group," she says. "I hope other women will try to do what I am doing. I have already interested some other widows in the idea. All it takes is a little sincere interest and spare time."

"I don't like to be referred to as a widow," remarked one recently during an interview regarding a certain matter. "Can't you come up with something better?"

"Why?" I asked, not at all surprised.

In trying to explain her feelings, she became a trifle tongue-tied, but finally blurted out: "I detest that word! It annoys me terribly."

"Well, to be truthful, I don't like it any better than

you do," I admitted, "and we're not the only ones. Maybe, someday, someone will coin a more pleasing term. Until then, we're stuck with it, I guess."

"And with widows, too," she added somewhat ruefully.

Analyzing her objection objectively, it appears that the onus bears not so much on the word "widow," as upon its connotation. The word is derived from the Latin *vidua*, which means to separate or divide. I used it once in an article to test reader-reaction. The first person who read it was an astute editor, and he gave it the blue-pencil treatment. In a subsequent article, I used "relict," another term for widow. It stems from the Latin *relictus*, meaning to leave behind or relinquish. Then I decided to forego it, for it could be confused with "relic," which, in some ways, is not a complimentary word. I have not found a suitable substitute. A name is a term which expresses some quality characteristic or descriptive of a thing. Considering the derivation and definition of "widow," it is difficult to find fault with the word.

As I write this section I am reminded of the woman who baked wonderful pies of many kinds. Inasmuch as her husband liked only mince and never knew which was what when he wanted to help himself, she invented a means of identification. The mince pies were marked with a T.M., meaning " 'Tis Mince." The others were marked with a T.M., meaning " 'Tain't Mince," and he was still in a quandary. That anecdote seems to sum up my position on the question—without mincing any more words.

SOCIAL ACTIVITY

She was an elderly woman, a widow having a light lunch at a midtown cafeteria. She smiled at the child sitting opposite her and asked: "How old are you, little girl?"

She was surprised when the child's mother replied: "Physically, she is ten; emotionally, she is seven; intellectually, she is fifteen; actually, she is nine."

A small smile from the elderly woman acknowledged the answer; then she retreated into a shell to contemplate her own age. "What am I?" she asked herself. "Seventy, or fifty, or eighty-five, or sixty-five?"

No one is one age. Everyone is several ages. Aging is a complicated process. It varies among individuals and within individuals, progressing at diverse rates in different parts of the body, altering mental and physical abilities. There is no specific date on which a person is suddenly precipitated into old age. Legally, we come of age the day we are twenty-one, and the event is accompanied by a feeling of satisfaction.

But eventually, a day will come when finally we will be forced to admit we have reached advanced age. With that awareness comes a feeling of shock. That is the day to start taking stock of our total situation, if we have not, as yet, done so. In our own interest and that of family, friends, and society in general, it is incumbent upon us to find the facts. To face the facts. To know where we are going. To know what we have to go on physically and financially. To examine our outlook on the future.

A good place to start is at the office of a good doctor for a complete physical checkup. The purpose is not to expect trouble, but to detect the start or state of possible disease so that it may be avoided or alleviated. That done, we should consider the matters of income and occupation. Generally most people want to keep usefully busy, whether or not they need the income. What do I have to live on? How much do I need? Where can I earn more, if necessary? What abilities do I have to offer that will produce a pay check, or personal satisfaction, or both? Each question is pertinent and provokes thought.

Few people wear out. Most of them vegetate and deteriorate mentally, as well as physically. So, it is important to have a hobby or an interest to abate the tedium of the passing days; to do the things one has always longed to do, or, lacking the means or the ability, to adopt a satisfactory substitute.

There are things to do that have genuine purpose, and things that offer more pleasure than purpose. The election is a personal matter and, as with other interests, the successful use of leisure requires planning. Some social activity is of paramount importance. There are few pleasures so satisfying as getting together with family and friends to engage in stimulating conversation, or to participate in some enjoyable activity.

As we grow older, we find it more difficult to maintain our social contacts. Many widows in particular long for a "good old-fashioned gabfest with the girls," and the effort to get together should be made if at all possible. For friends and friendship are important to peace of mind, and particularly for oldsters who live alone.

There is no good reason why we should not make good use of our later years. They are the culmination of life. So let's live them.

REGARDING REMARRIAGE

Assuming a widow is disposed to remarry, what are her chances? Hopeful? Or doubtful? Will dependent children, social position, racial extraction, or economic condition improve or impair her opportunity? Will her age and the time elapsed since she entered widowhood have any bearing on the matter of remarriage?

Put any of those questions to any number of persons picked at random, and expect to receive as many different answers, all of them guesses, few of them good. But factual answers are available in a report of the Proceedings of the Casualty Actuarial Society which contained an American Remarriage Table together with explanatory matter detailed to an extraordinary degree.

The table was constructed on the basis of assembled experience covering a period of nineteen years, and represents individual observation of more than

10,500 cases. The report was limited to widows who became beneficiaries under the workmen's compensation laws in states where their status as beneficiaries changes with remarriage.

Study of the table and of the explanatory text reveals that during the early years of widowhood, the duration of widowhood may have a greater effect on the remarriage rate than the age of the widow. The experience beyond the sixth year of widowhood was so limited that the actuaries decided to eliminate it from the calculations altogether. That is significant! It indicates that if a widow does not remarry within the first five or six years of her bereavement, she is not likely to remarry after that period.

At any age of entry into widowhood, according to the table, a certain percentage of women remarry within the year of bereavement. The younger the age-group, the higher the rate of remarriage. The remarriage rate—at any age—reaches a peak-point during the following year, after the formal period of respect has elapsed. During the second and the third years, the rates drop considerably, but remain approximately the same within each period. In the fourth year, the decline is very definite through the mid-life ages.

In the fifth year, and beyond, the rate is even lower than it was during the period prior to the first full year of bereavement.

One good guess was ratified by the report. It shows that, the percentage possibility of remarriage decreases surely and steadily . . . as age increases. As a matter of fact, fewer than 3 per cent of the women who became widows in any one year are likely to remarry within five or six years.

That percentage applied to the annual average of 450,000 new widows indicates that approximately 1,300 cases may result in remarriage.

As to the effect of dependent children on the possibility of remarriage, the investigation indicated that that factor was too small to give reliable results. However, there seemed to be a slight tendency for the rate to vary inversely with the number of children.

The influence of social position, racial stock, economic condition, and also the effect of a lump sum allowance (or dowry) upon remarriage seemed to make no material difference. This information was obtained after a long and diligent search. Before it became available, the Dutch and Danish remarriage tables were considered to be the standard sources of information on the subject. Obviously, based on American experience, this information is more reliable for those who have a personal or professional interest in a widow's chances for remarriage. Statistically, at least, it seems to be a case of now or never.

What ideas would impel a man to marry a much younger woman—a widow? What incentives would induce a widow to marry a much younger man? What exceptional problems are apt to be encountered by the parties to such a union? What may be termed a "mis-matched" marriage?

It is easier to "separate the wheat from the chaff" than it is to separate abnormal from normal marriage by reason of age difference. It may be set down as a fact that the behavior patterns of the individuals constituting the couple are apt to differ in direct ratio to their age differential.

First, perhaps, custom should be considered. Society not only sanctions, but expects the husband to be senior to the wife to a reasonable extent. Second, the greater the *numerical* age-gap between them, the more certain is the possibility that the marriage will be complicated with problems. Third, the greater the *natural* age-gap with respect to their individual ages, the greater is the likelihood that the problems will be pronounced in character. Obviously, a husband of 38 and a wife of 18 would probably have more acute problems than a husband of 60 and a wife of 40. While in each case the *actual* age differential is twenty years, the *essential* age-ratio of the husband to the wife in the first case is more than 2 to 1; while in the second case, the age-ratio is 1.5 to 1. Ignoring temperamental and considering only mathematical factors, the older couple has a much better chance for marital happiness.

A number of the special reasons which cause people, both widows and wooers, of abnormal age difference to seek marriage are basically similar. One or the other, unable to secure a mate of compatible age, and loath to continue living alone, will, in sheer desperation, accept a person of disproportionate age. One or the other may be emotionally embryonic to the extent that a parent substitute is sought, rather than a spouse as such. One or the other may want an aged spouse in order to avoid children or additional children. In this matter, for biological reasons, the man has greater assurance than the woman. While her reproductive powers will terminate at some point in her life, his may continue as long as he lives.

One or the other may succumb to adulation. Assuming that an older man "knows women and their ways," the woman may be flattered by the fact that such a man found her more alluring than all others. The younger man may be complimented by the fact that a "woman of some experience" chose him to the exclusion of all other possible suitors.

One or the other may be animated by a desire to dominate. While the younger person may gratify the animus through the older spouse's gratitude for a younger mate, the older person may satisfy this yearning because of his advanced age and acumen acquired through long experience.

One or the other may desire a young spouse who is unusually attractive physically, therefore more stimulating as a mate. While this propensity may be more general among men than among women, a number of well-publicized widows have been accused of "cradle-snatching."

Since tradition frowns upon the marriage of an older woman and a younger man, the persons constituting such a union have a considerable problem of adjusting themselves to a public as well as to a private attitude. If people pry, poke fun, look askance, and regard such a union as "freaky," about the only thing a couple so situated can do is assume a sensible attitude and adhere to a steadfast faith in the propriety and security of their relationship.

FIFTH WHEEL ON THE WAGON

A young society matron lost her wealthy, important, and popular husband recently. How he met his end is not important here. When he was alive they lived the good life, traveled widely, entertained and were entertained lavishly, and were the center, or close to the center of most of the city's major social splurges.

Now, for all the difference it makes to anyone, even those she regards as her closest friends, "the earth opened and swallowed her alive," along with her dead husband, as she puts it graphically, if not elegantly. There have been a few invitations to luncheon from some of the girls, and an occasional invitation to dinner at their homes, but as far as the social whirl is concerned—well, she has been whirled out of it. She wonders and worries, and wants to know why she is being banished.

Apparently the friends of this worldly woman had greater regard for the aspects of the situation than she had and still has. During the earlier months of her bereavement, she would be expected to retire almost completely from conspicuous social activity. For one thing, to give her time to regain her composure. For another, out of respect to her deceased husband. And for still another, perhaps, not to overtax her probably impaired vitality during a time when so many difficult details concerning estate-settlement would claim her attention.

Now that period has passed and she is still ostracized from social affairs. She may not like to admit it, but she lost her biological significance when she lost her husband. Generally, living things—male and female—pair off for a period of time, in some species for life, and she was the female who was paired with a male in the human species. With respect to "hen parties," she is a free agent. In regard to affairs which require an approved male escort she is not. That's the way it is, and that's the way it may be until doomsday for all anyone knows. The average human being is such a conformist in matters of dress and deportment that he'd rather *be* ridiculous than *look* ridiculous. He is reluctant to depart from custom, and to permit others to do so. Popular opinion forces some relaxation, but with limitations. Complete release may look like something so idealistic it may never be attained.

ROBERTA'S DILEMMA

Roberta's boy friend seems to be clever with "the lie that binds." She wants him to marry her. He is stubborn. They have come to an impasse. She seeks advice.

To recapitulate the situation: Her husband passed away eight years ago. She had had no thought of ever marrying again. Then she met Jerry. That happened one afternoon when she made a professional visit to his office. Roberta and Jerry were attracted to each other immediately.

It was late in the day. They lived in the same direction. It was about time to close up shop anyway, so he offered to take her to her home. She accepted. During the drive he mentioned that he was divorced, lonesome, and that he would like to see her socially as well as professionally. Lonesome herself, and charmed by Jerry's personality and professional position, Roberta accepted, with alacrity, an invitation to have dinner with him that very evening.

Soon, they were "going steady," and "going strong." She admits that one evening, unable to repress her feelings, she practically proposed to him. Thereupon he told her that he had no intention of ever marrying again; he explained that his first marriage had been such a miserable experience that he was fearful of venturing a second. But he would love to continue the affair on a "boy friend" basis. After they knew each other better—well, possibly he might change his mind.

Now she is frantic because she fears that their friendship is on the verge of becoming unplatonic. She vows she won't give in, or give him up. And he won't budge. That's the status quo. It would seem that if bothered and bewildered Roberta means to preserve her purity, that ought to end her dilemma. Mentally, she resolved the relationship when she resolved to be "a good girl." Therefore, the physical break should not be too painful because she is totally right.

It is a fair assumption that what Roberta wants is not advice, but a measure of impersonal moral(e) support. And now, she has it. However, it would be well to consider a possible corollary development that could be danger-laden. For fear of losing her, Jerry might induce himself to enter into a sanctioned relationship. In that event, would she, would he, would they have hoped-for happiness of a high order?

Once divorced, would a possible second experience be of serious concern to Jerry? As for Roberta, would she want to chance the possibility of being a grass widow as well as a sod widow? Often the best answer to a question is a more comprehensive question.

SAMANTHA

Something told me Samantha might be a widow, but there was nothing in her demeanor to indicate that she might be a three-time loser. Employed as a saleslady in a store owned by a man I knew, she had waited on me several times in the past. On this occasion, she helped me select a gift for a friend. Samantha was wrapping the purchase when the owner approached me and said, "I see your column is now nationally syndicated; how's it going?"

"Very well, indeed," I was able to say. "It's running in newspapers from coast to coast and from Canada to Texas."

"Well, it should be well received," he observed. "It makes sense. It's certainly needed, Lord knows, considering what's happening to so many men."

I thanked him, took the package from Samantha and started to leave when he said, "You two ought to know each other better; I mean to exchange ideas. There aren't many women who've been through what this little lady has experienced."

"Then you are a widow," I said to Samantha. "I thought you might be."

But her boss answered for her: "Not once or twice, but three times."

Speechless with surprise, I turned to Samantha for verification. A wan smile and a slight nod said, "Yes, that is true."

After a faltering pause, I said, "I'm sorry," and Samantha said, "Some of your articles have been very helpful to me. I read them regularly. If nothing more they are showing people that there are a lot of widows with a lot of problems in the world."

"But what about yours?" I asked. "How are you managing? It would seem that you, in particular, would have a great deal to contend with."

"Well, I did have," she replied, "but I finally gained control of myself and after that it wasn't so bad. Losing three husbands in eighteen years demoralized me.

They were all killed in automobile accidents, and I was almost killed myself in the last one.

"I thought I was a jinx. I didn't want to live. People told me to pray for help. I did, but I was too hurt in body and soul to care. All I had to look forward to was doctor bills, hospitals bills, and a big law suit. And terrible memories."

"You must have received encouragement from some source," I said.

"Yes, I did," she agreed. "From my stepchildren. I have no children of my own, but my last two husbands had children I love very much, and they love me.

"My eldest stepdaughter and her husband gave up their home, work and everything and came to take care of me. When I left the hospital, they decided to remain here, and I live with them. All of my stepchildren helped me in every way they could, just as if I were their real mother. For that, I thanked God, and that's when my prayers began to have meaning. As you see, I lived through it all, and I am trying to be a good mother to the children of the men I was married to."

Before I left, I asked Samantha which one of the men to whom she had been married meant most to her.

"I loved each one for what he was," she answered with assurance. "They were fine men, all of them."

That is the story of Samantha whose life was thrice disrupted and restored. The woman who fears she lost everything when she lost her husband would do well to take it to mind and to heart.

**THE WIDOW WHO
WON'T REMARRY**

No one who assumes the responsibility of writing a book of this nature can hope to compress everything that merits attention into eight chapters. Or into eighty, for that matter. At times, he finds himself behind or beyond his agenda. Then he must stop and take stock of the situation.

An inventory of the topics already discussed and yet to be considered indicates that thought is now due the widow who can remarry, but who refuses to do so because she feels she would not be faithful to the memory of her late husband.

Some months before these lines were written, I found myself sharing a bus seat with an unknown woman. In order to test an idiosyncrasy again—an acquired ability to identify a widow almost immediately, or after a few words of conversation—I engaged the lady in innocuous chitchat. Very soon she volunteered the information that she was employed as a salesperson in a department store. That she was almost too worn out to go to work. That she regretted now that she had not been more reasonable and less reluctant about a certain matter some years ago. Sensing that my fellow-passenger was looking for an opportunity to unburden her feelings, I asked a few leading questions which resulted in replies that were replete with information.

As I surmised, she was a widow. Lost her husband

nine years ago. His last illness and the funeral expenses left her almost destitute. She had no children. She was obliged to find work immediately to support herself and pay accumulated bills. She was tired out and terribly lonely. She lived alone in a small furnished room, and took her meals here, there, and everywhere. Her only local relative was a bachelor brother-in-law who took little interest in her. She realized she looked years older than her actual age.

She sat in silence for a while, then mentioned she could have married a well-to-do former suitor seven years ago, but had refused to do so because of a feeling of fidelity with respect to her late husband. Reminded that even the marriage rite took no account of her conduct after her husband's death and demanded faithfulness of her only until his passing obliterated the oath, I asked her, "Did the religious release carry no weight with you?"

"None whatever," was her reply. "That is, not until recently, and maybe not even now. I'm not sure. Some women are like that, I guess." And with that, she picked up her belongings and left the bus.

This faithfulness, this fidelity to a departed spouse, is impelled by an inordinate moral emotion which is not sanctioned by religious scruples or common sense.

In the New Testament, we learn of Paul saying in his letters to the Corinthians (I): *I say therefore to the unmarried and to the widows, it is good for them if they abide even as I. But if they cannot contain, let them marry; for it is better to marry than to burn.*

The wife is bound by the laws as long as the husband liveth; but if her husband be dead, she is at liberty to be married to whom she will; only in the Lord.

The marriage vows state explicitly that the contracting parties shall love and honor each other "until death do you part." There is no obligation, written or implied, beyond the first relationship. Assuming that any stoppage to a second marriage has been resolved, does that mean that a widow should leap without looking into the arms of the first available suitor because marriageable men are comparatively scarce? Not the wary widow! The same impediments which would have been inimical to the success of the first marriage may involve the second. Therefore, they should again receive careful pre-marital consideration.

WITH COURAGE AND COMMON SENSE

Americans are a marrying nation. In 1955, according to a census report, 76 per cent of all the households in our nation were husband-wife domiciles. At the same time, however, an average of 1,300 marriages a day are disrupted by death of the husband. Two per cent are disjoined while husband and wife are yet half-strangers to each other. About 8 per cent are severed during those years when the couples are learning to pull together as a team. Slightly fewer than 40 per cent are disunited when wedlock is in the full rich bloom of mature love.

Fifty per cent are broken apart during those ages

when the years have mellowed marriage to a state of mutual satisfaction and solicitude. Obviously, the age of the wife when she enters widowhood will be a principal factor in the problem of managing a second readjustment. Upon her bereavement, the widow of 24 will not contemplate her situation with the comparative composure that will characterize one of 74. The younger woman releases her attachment with rebellious reluctance, while the older woman does so with calm resignation.

The younger widow will struggle to subdue her feminine feelings, while the older woman will strive to silence the aches and pains which denote the inevitable deterioration of her physical powers. The affectionate, husband-hungry woman of 34 will crave the company of some sympathetic man to punctuate the tedium of her monotonous todays and tomorrows, while the amiable person of 54 will cherish the company of almost anyone who may help her lessen the desolation of her declining years. Suffering the loss of her beloved spouse the woman of quiet temperament may become mute with mourning. She stores her despair deeply and deplores silently within her desolate heart.

But the gnawing grief of another will not permit her to placate her feelings. She becomes a mourning-dove, lamenting audibly: "Why did this have to have to happen to me?" And what is there of practical worth in trying to placate her with pleasing platitudes? She should accept the answer she invites. For example: "Would you rather that it happened to any other woman who is near and dear to you?

"From among all the wives in the land, why were you singled out for this tribulation? It happens to 30,000 women a month. Suppose that occasionally and perhaps often, they did taste some marital strife together with sweetness, were their husband less desirable to them than yours was to you?"

Given courage and common sense, a widow may face the future philosophically. Living gracefully, with consideration for herself and for all others, in all respects, she will live usefully, and she will bring honor to womanhood collectively, and to widowhood specifically.

All over the land, communities offer their citizens, at least those of Christian faith, opportunity for religious worship in churches of their choice. By just about every means of mass communication, people are invited, even exhorted to attend church. Yet, a number of elderly widows have told me that they are not able to avail themselves of the religious and social values of church attendance due to two deterrents: They don't go to church as often as they used to because they can't afford to put money on the collection plate, and because of transportation difficulties.

Those reasons were revealed by a survey conducted by the Community Welfare Service of Long Beach. Questionnaires were sent to a cross-section of the city's 30,000 elderly persons. Using recent census figures and a slide rule, I came to the conclusion that some 2,000 of the elderly folks, age 65 and older, were widows. The same ratio should apply substantially to the people of almost any community who are similarly affected. Still, it is difficult to see why transportation difficulties and low income, combined with social pressure for financial support of the churches, should prevent church attendance by elderly retired people. May I remind my readers of the widow's mite, a small gift or contribution freely given by one who can scarcely afford it?

In Mark 12:41-44 it is written: *And Jesus sat against the treasury, and beheld how the people cast money into the treasury, and many that were rich cast in much.*

And there came a certain poor widow, and she threw in two mites, which made a farthing.

And He called unto him his disciples, and saith unto them, Verily I say unto you, that this poor widow hath cast more in, than all they which have cast into the treasury. For all they had cast in of their abundance; but she of her want cast in all that she had, even all her living.

Which is to say, in the vernacular, that the dime which a poor widow may put on the collection plate is larger in the eyes of the Lord than the dollar or two which a person better situated may put on the plate.

As for transportation, I am sure that any person who has difficulty in that respect need only notify the minister of the church, and he will see to it that it will be provided by members of the congregation.

Mrs. J. W. P., a widow, thinks she has lived too long. She is so hurt that she is not interested in learning where she stands legally in a rather sordid situation. The Division of Aid for the Aged found a home for her with another widow, also a pensioner. And so she lives her dreary days.

Situations in which a widow will take other persons into her home for economic and/or social reasons are common enough. Often, the other persons are relatives. Quite frequently the arrangement is mutually satisfactory. Yet, there is always the possibility that someone will take advantage of the situation.

This case involves the widow in question, her nephew, his wife, and his stepson. When her nephew's parents lost their lives in a tragic accident, she took him into her home. She treated him like a son—sheltered, clothed, fed him, and provided for his education. After graduation, he left to work in a distant city. He remained away for years. In spite of all that his aunt had done for him, he ignored her completely. One day he returned with his family. They moved in without even saying as much as "by your leave," and made themselves at home, as the saying goes.

The widow did not resent the encroachment. In fact, she welcomed the intruders, for she was lonely, ailing, and ill-off financially. They would make things better for her, she thought. Of her own volition, she deeded her home to her nephew, provided he would care for her the rest of her days. But soon she found that she was little more than a stranger, a servant, in the home that was once hers.

Her nephew was improvident; his wife, indolent; their son, insolent. Each indulged himself in his own way and increased her work and her worries to a trying extent. Unknown to her, they borrowed all they could get on the home and used the proceeds to buy an old car and new clothes. They never invited her to go with them on their pleasure jaunts. She, too, needed clothes, but they didn't buy her a stitch.

Unable to meet the mortgage payments, the "squander bugs" revealed their duplicity and urged the widow to take in lodgers to raise the money.

When she refused to agree to that unreasonable demand, they told her to get out. All wrought up, she raised such a ruckus that they got out themselves.

Eventually, the property was sold to satisfy the mortgage. She was all but helpless when she had to give up the home she had worked hard to help her husband buy—the home she had lived in for almost twenty years.

In making this revelation, there is no intent to sow seeds of suspicion. But it is never amiss to be circumspect. It is possible to avoid many aggravating experiences by being cautious and prudent.

To me, the ways in which widows are wronged by others is a fairly familiar story; the ways in which they wrong themselves, and often others, is a source of never-ending wonder.

I cite three cases which have come to my attention. To cloak the identities of the women involved, I shall call them Mrs. Ann Ticipation, Mrs. Ann Archy, and Mrs. Ann O'Yance.

To Mrs. Ann Ticipation I said, "Was widowhood so abhorrent to you and the possibilities of remarriage so meager that you were willing to pay such a stiff premium to insure yourself another husband?

"Many widows are taken in by welshers. Assuming the intentions of your intended were honest and above board, was it wise of you to give him $1,200 without first obtaining commensurate security, or any legally acceptable assurance of repayment?

"Unfortunately, he dropped dead of a heart attack, so you'll never know his true worth. You wonder what chance you have to recover your loss. So do I. Considering the circumstance, I wouldn't think your chances are too good. I suggest you engage an able attorney to investigate the possibilities, and file a claim against the estate, if it would warrant your doing so."

To Mrs. Ann Archy I said, "Why do you oppose your employer? He gave you a good, well-paying job. He runs a successful business and should know what the score is. So, when it's necessary for you to sign letters, sign them as he wants you to, or you may be looking for another job with prospects of facing the same self-made problem.

"As a matter of fact, your employer is right. As a widow, you continue to use your late husband's given name socially, and your own given name in legal and financial matters. But it is not obligatory for you to use 'Mrs.' when signing a letter for your employer. Does he sign his letters with 'Mr.' before his name? Hardly! Instead of using their given and middle names, business women quite properly use only their initials and surnames. Generally, employers favor that style of signature to avoid any possible feeling of prejudice on the part of the recipient when it is apparent that the letter was written by a woman."

To a daughter of Mrs. Ann O'Yance I said, "Of course your mother dearly loves her many grandchildren and derives great pleasure from giving them nice birthday and holiday gifts. However, if she is spoiling them on the one hand through overindulgence, and denying herself on the other through overspending, then you do have cause for concern. And the subterfuges you and your sisters must resort to to reimburse her do not help the situation.

"Grandmothers generally regard themselves as highly privileged persons with regard to their grandchildren. Within reasonable limits that is good, but they have no right to assume the role of part-time matriarchs, uttering ultimatums.

"Try tactfully to have your mother moderate her attitude and her gift-giving ideas. Open her eyes to the fact that genuine happiness is exchanged, not given."

Widows and widowers are troubled less by recurring headaches than single, married, separated, or divorced persons. That was revealed in a report of the most extensive medical study ever made of one of mankind's most prevalent disorders. But I doubt if any persons are more troubled by the "headaches" that "trigger" headaches than those who are widowed, and the vast majority of them are worried women.

The foregoing and the following paragraphs have been written in behalf of Mrs. H. P. S., and any other widow who is or may be confronted with a similar "headache."

You say you have been a widow for two years and that your late husband's business partner, who is now your business partner, wants to marry you. Your children are grown and have gone elsewhere to live their own lives. You do not like to live alone without a husband's love.

You admit you have always had a "soft spot" in your heart for your suitor and would marry him in a minute if it were not for one drawback: the fundamental difference in your religious faiths. Furthermore, you reveal that that concern has become complicated with another headache: if you will not marry the man in question, he intends to dispose of his interest in the business and leave town. He cannot maintain the close business contact with you, which is essential, and contain his personal feelings at the same time.

You cannot operate the business without him and

you are doubly distressed. You want to know if such a marriage would work out. For what it's worth, this is what I think:

Generally, a mixed marriage of any nature could encounter difficulties, especially when the couple is young and children may ensue. But in your case, the probability of children and the problems of their religious upbringing need hardly be considered. And with fortitude and finesse, you should be able to overcome the social obstacles others may use to harass you.

If you are emotionally mature enough to control your conduct, come what may, your faith in yourself and in your suitor should provide a secure foundation for a successful marriage—provided each of you understands and respects the fundamental precepts of the other's religious adherence.

However, a word of caution with respect to another factor intrudes upon my thinking about your case. You may have a soft spot in your heart for your suitor, but be sure you don't have one in your head. Considering his ultimatum, I am wondering if he is trying, through marriage, to maneuver himself into a position that may enable him to effect greater or complete control of the business.

Ask yourself that question and try to come up with a carefully considered answer. I do not mean to plant suspicions in your mind. I am merely suggesting that you temper the warm spot in your heart with some cool-headed thinking.

MEMORANDUM ON MEMORIALS

"My husband passed away only a few months ago, and already some of his relatives are telling me what kind of a monument they expect me to place on his grave," laments Mrs. A. L. F.

"According to my religion, it is an obligation for me to take care of this by the first anniversary of his death, and I will. Naturally, this is a sad responsibility for me, and I don't see why they should add to my sorrow by dictating to me what kind of a monument it should be, especially when they have not offered to share any part of the cost.

"They have shown me some pictures of expensive stones. They have decided on one they like very much. But I don't like it for two reasons. In the first place, it's too showy and in the second, it's too expensive. Aaron was a plain, thrifty, sensible man, and I

217

am sure he would not want me to make a splurge for
his sake, even for a monument in his memory.

"I have talked it over with my only son, and he
seems to agree with his uncles and aunts, so I would
really appreciate your advice. Should I do what I
think is right, or what they think I ought to do?"

Considering the circumstances of your case, Mrs.
F., I am in complete accord with you from every
standpoint. To my knowledge, there is no requirement
that holds the people of your faith or any faith to the
expenditure of a certain amount of money for a monument. Nor are there any conditions with respect to its
dimensions or design. The matter of choice is a personal matter entirely, and in your particular case, you
should be permitted to make the decision without
criticism.

I would counsel a modest marker with the suggestion that, if possible, its cost be matched with an
equal sum to be donated to some worthy cause in
memory of your husband.

The tradition which relates to the marking of graves
may be traced to remote antiquity. Perceivably, primitive man placed heavy stones and other markings on
graves, not only to keep the evil spirits which he
thought dwelt in dead bodies from escaping, but also
to mark the spot as a place to be avoided.

Centuries later the custom still prevailed, but the
philosophy had changed. Three different ideas provided incentive for erecting monuments to the de-

parted: 1) A belief that the body abides or sleeps in the place prepared for it. 2) To indicate the place where the remains of a person of special attainment were interred. 3) The provision of a stone or a tablet beseeching the prayers of co-religionists for the repose of a departed soul.

Today's incentive is provided by the popular notion that the erection of some sort of a monument is a necessary concluding phase of the funeral ceremony. In many cases, a mingling of personal, social, and commercial pressures inspires expenditures for monuments that are extravagant beyond an amount that is warranted or affordable. By such ideas are individuals burdened with expenditures that in the aggregate represent an enormous amount of money. Much of it would serve a far more useful purpose if it were devoted to the erection of charitable institutions and organizations for the care of the ill and the indigent. And to the support of educational institutions.

Community foundations through which various gifts and bequests for community betterment and other purposes may be distributed have been established in a number of cities.

The purpose of the community foundation is to effect distribution of income from a combined number of modest individual gifts, in the same manner that benefits are distributed from a single munificent fund. Control is complete, and intelligent, centralized administration permits employment of such funds in the most beneficial manner, in the light of ever-changing conditions.

When the donor specifies that his benefaction is to serve a particular purpose, approval of the allotment is a mere formality. When the gift is not restricted, the distribution committee tells the trustee how the income is to be employed. Intended monument money used in this manner would mean much more to mankind than the millions of stereotyped statements chiseled in untold tons of cold metal and marble. Given in the names of departed persons, it would mean many more of those worthy civic, charitable, and educational institutions which are essential to the welfare of humanity. And it would make for far better employment of the durable materials and skillful manpower that are involved.

Slowly, sometimes faintly and falteringly, but always onward and upward, the line that marks the course of human progress creeps from century to century. The community foundation, which permits those of modest means as well as those of wealth to participate in projects for community betterment, is a long step taken in the right direction—in an enlightened direction. The idea of the memorial park, as an ideal environment in which to inter the remains of the departed, is another. Both conceptions are commendable in that they take into account consideration for others as well as for oneself.

The memorial park, which is gaining ground in the environs of a number of large cities, is a far cry from the old-style cemetery. Beholding the one, the on-looker "cannot see the monuments for the forest of stone," so to speak. Contemplating the other, he cannot see the graves for the unobstructed vistas of scenic beauty which stretch before him. Here, all lie on a common level, beneath the sod and *above* the sod. Decent disposal is accorded the dead in a parkland from which only objectionable elements have been removed and to which only befitting enhancements have been added.

Each grave is identified by means of a simple inexpensive bronze marker, of standard size and design. This requirement results in several definite advantages: 1) Simple, dignified, unassuming identification, similar to the modesty of the military cemetery. 2) Commendable, and, in many cases, essential economy. 3) No neglected graves, for no plot offers an obstructing monument to interfere with the efficient mechanized equipment which is used to mow the meadow-like burial areas. Neglect and natural growth of grass and weeds are not permitted to obliterate the graves. No cemetery should be an eye-sore, and too many are.

Several writers have suggested the use of a memorial tree to substitute for the cold and costly stone memorial. In one way and another, they have unknowingly endorsed the stand taken here, and have advanced sound suggestions of their own which are entirely sympathetic to this discussion.

In any event, one's conscience and one's circumstances will control individual conduct in the matter of a memorial, even as these considerations measure the election of and the expenditure for other mortuary merchandise and service.

To live in the hearts we leave behind is a memorial that cannot be contrived through expenditure of any amount of money for a mundane memorial.